HEAVENLY AMBASSADORS IN THE MAKING

BECOMING *the* PERSON YOU WERE CREATED *to* BE

by

GREG ALLENBY, BENJAMIN GRAHAM,
AND TIMOTHY WAMBURA

Heaven's Ambassadors in the Making:
Becoming the Person You Were Created to Be

Copyright © 2020 by Greg Allenby, Benjamin Graham, and Timothy Wambura

Published by Deep River Books
Sisters, Oregon
www.deepriverbooks.com

Cover design by Jason Enterline

ISBN—13: 9781632695314
Library of Congress Control Number: 2020910301

Printed in the USA
2020—First Edition

29 28 27 26 25 24 23 22 21 20   10 9 8 7 6 5 4 3 2 1

TABLE OF CONTENTS

PREFACE

Timothy and Happiness Wambura were going to a church conference held in Springfield, Missouri five years ago, and travelled through Columbus, Ohio, visiting supporters of their orphanages and schools in Africa. They needed a place to stay, and the Allenbys had bedrooms that weren't being used because their children were grown and out of the house. The first meeting between the Wamburas and Greg and Tricia Allenby produced a friendship that continues to grow today as they do God's work.

The Allenbys are involved in prison ministry. They own and operate two houses—Covenant House and Fort Jackson in Columbus, Ohio—that serve as places for men to transition to freedom. Men learn about the houses from the prison chaplains, church services, and a newsletter that goes into prison to tell men there are people who care about them and want to help them reconnect with their families, find employment, and become productive members of society. The editor of the newsletter, Benjamin Graham, also serves as house manager of Covenant House. Benjamin is a poet laureate—a fact that becomes evident as you read his poetry in this book.

The Wamburas are involved with two orphanages in Arusha, Tanzania. Camp Moses is for preschool children who are destitute, many of them abandoned by their parents because of poverty and alcoholism. Camp Joshua is for students in primary school and is located near the slums of Unga Limited in Arusha. They also have a clinic/hospital in Shinyanga, Tanzania for the elderly and disadvantaged, and a leadership school near Lake Victoria in the Rorya district of Tanzania, where many people have not yet heard the gospel message.

We have found much commonality in our ministries. This probably shouldn't be surprising, because we are both striving for the same goal. Nonetheless, the universality of God's message has struck us as something we want to talk about together. The commands of Jesus and God's call on our lives are the same, whether you are a destitute child in Africa or a transitioning prisoner in Ohio. Our struggle with temptation is common.

We view the transition houses, orphanages, schools, and hospitals in our ministries as embassies of heaven. They are outposts in a foreign land and are staffed by ambassadors for Christ. Our goal is to develop heaven's ambassadors by providing safe places where the Holy Spirit can operate, allowing the individuals who come to us to work out what God has already given them. This book describes how we go about accomplishing this task.

You will find our descriptions of the human condition to be loving, perplexing, appalling, sad, happy, and just about any other adjective you might want to add to this list. As we often say in the prison ministry, "You can't make this stuff up." Both of our ministries are at the front line of the war between good and evil, somewhere between heaven and hell, as people struggle with their identity, their past, and their desire for a better life.

The chapters of our book represent a progression for the development of heaven's ambassadors. The first step (Chapter 1) is to come to Christ; the remaining steps build upon that. The sequence is not fixed, as some people may experience a deepening of their faith in a different order than expressed here; but generally speaking, one can't be an effective role model (Chapter 10) without first learning first to be a servant (Chapter 3).

All of the book chapters are based on the teachings of Christ. As you read, we encourage you to think about the ministries you are involved with and see if they can be improved with what Jesus has taught us. We hope you are motivated to see your role as an ambassador of heaven.

Timothy is an ordained minister in the Assemblies of God Church, and Greg is a professor at Ohio State University. All of us (Greg, Benjamin, and Timothy) have a heart for the lost and neglected, and we work for the spiritual development of the of the individuals who come to us. We hope you enjoy reading about our experiences and think about how our stories relate to you and your story.

What Is Your Vision?

In times gone by, I've seen myself
    as a number of different things . . .
From a superman to a movie star
    to a "player" with many "rings"

I've seen myself as a family man
    with a home and a great big yard
With a lovely wife and scholarly kids . . .
    as a man who worked real hard

I've seen myself as an entrepreneur
    owning businesses . . . (more than one)
I've seen myself as a game-show host
    having lots and lots of fun

I dreamed of being an inventor
    (and I have an invention or two)
I've had visions of being a rich man . . .
    And I guess you've had those, too

But now I see things differently . . .
    since God has changed my vision
With less fantasy . . . less vanity . . .
    less spiritual "collision" (Isaiah 43:19)

Less focus on the worldly things
    that feed into my pride
More focus on the "Spirit" . . .
    that guides me from "inside" (John 16:3)

Today I have a vision
    of affecting how folks think
Proclaiming and declaring
    that . . . life doesn't have to stink

Speaking out to hearts and minds
    of all those who will listen
That if you don't know the God we serve . . .
    you don't know what you're missin'

Today I have a vision
    that foresees God's church . . . united (Acts 2:46)
Quickened from those things to which
    we all were once acquainted

Disregarding that old man . . .
　　that we need now forget
Reaching for that perfect one
　　who paid for us our debt

Of being God's ambassador
　　(to which we all are called)
Abandoning that life which
　　had us formerly enthralled

Have you a vision now . . . today,
　　that God has surely given? (Acts 2:17)
Something you desire to do
　　while still among the livin'?

To preach or teach or somehow reach
　　the souls that may be lost
To shine your light in darkness . . .
　　not to worry what it cost?

God gave us all our special skill . . .
　　at something you're a *whiz*! (Deuteronomy 28:12–13)
You just need to take the time
　　to find out what it is

Make manifest your vision friends,
　　see yourself as *great*! (1 Peter 2:9)
Explore your great potential . . . now! . . .
　　before it gets too late.

Chapter 1

HOW IT STARTS

There was a known witchdoctor in the ward of Raranya for quite a long time, and people trusted him for what he did for them. African belief in witchcraft is still very strong. Almost everything good or bad is associated with witchcraft. In other words, witchcraft in Africa has replaced God the Creator in people's minds and beliefs. Excelling or having misfortunes in life like being rich or poor, passing or failing the exams, getting promotions or being fired, doing well in business or experiencing a downfall, or being sick or dying are all associated with witchcraft.

Traditionally, even for one to get married or have a child would also be associated with witchcraft. A person would be advised to consult the witchdoctor for sorcery and see whether he/she should be married to the person he/she think to marry. The cultural system of Raranya has a spirit that is not connected to God. People go to witchdoctors to seek the answers for the desires they have. Unfortunately, the witchdoctors also have the way they play their games to make people who come to them feel that their problems are being solved by them. But at the end of the day, they find themselves in greater problems than before that requires them to seek another witchdoctor, who also does not solve the problem instead makes things worse.

The witchdoctor had lots of tools at home he was using. He was a crowd-puller; many people went to him to seek answers for their problems, and he used his witchcraft tools to deceive them.

In 2018, as I (Timothy) was preaching in the Tanzania Assemblies of God (TAG) church World Outreach Mission—Raranya, this witchdoctor came into the church. I could see him following keenly what I was preaching. It was during Easter service, and this man who appeared to be very prominent in that village took his time listening attentively to the message about the crucifixion of Christ.

At the end of the message, when I called for those who wanted to give their lives to Christ, the witchdoctor stood up and came straight to the pulpit, ready to repent and give his life to Christ. It was not an easy decision for an adult African male—especially one who was a very famous witchdoctor in that area—to walk openly down the church aisle, before adult males and females as well as children. It required a person to be really been touched by the power of God.

I asked him what he wanted, and he replied, "I want to repent for all I have been doing as a witchdoctor, and other sins. I want to accept Jesus Christ and declare Him to be my Master and Savior." As he was talking, I could see tears rolling out of his eyes, coming down the cheeks and dropping on the floor. He was ready. He knelt down, then repented, and accepted Jesus Christ as his Savior and Master.

It was a one-hundred-eighty-degree turnaround. The moment he repented and accepted Jesus Christ to be his Master and Savior, he came back to his senses, and asked the pastor of that area and his church elders to go to his home to burn all his witchcraft stuff. Immediately, after coming to Jesus, he realized that what he was holding at home were not valuables but Satan's tools. I recorded the scenario; we could see feathers of different birds, bones of different kinds of animals, and other horrible stuff.

> Becoming an ambassador starts with coming to Jesus and turning away from sin.

Come to Me

Come to me, all you who are weary and burdened, and I will give you rest.

(Matthew 11:28)

One of the truths that we hold in our ministries is that God does the heavy lifting. If men are not seeking God, there isn't much we can do for them. The Bible serves as the great common denominator for instruction and hope as people seek to change their lives. It introduces God as the loving and just God who demands obedience and yet offers grace through Jesus Christ.

The effect of this is that it allows us, as ambassadors of heaven, to walk beside those to whom we minister. We are not the judge, because God has already judged. We are not the solution, because the solution has already been offered. The intent of our actions is not to have people be like us, but for us to be like Jesus. We therefore do not need to act as rule-bearers and enforcers; we simply need to open up the Bible and see what God has to say about things.

The men coming to our (Greg's) prison ministry must fill out an application while in prison and be recommended by the prison chaplain. We especially want people to join us who have exhibited some priority for God in their lives while being incarcerated. One of the questions on our application form is "When did you come to saving faith?" and we leave five blank lines on the application form for men to respond. Sometimes all we get is a date like "October 2, 2010" and nothing else, and sometimes we get more than five lines of detailed description of what was happening in the life of the applicant. You would think that someone who understands who God is would want to tell everyone what He's done for them, and that all five lines on the form would be filled in. You might also assume that someone that just gives a date is "faking it" and is just looking to avoid the homeless shelter. Unfortunately, neither is true.

Everyone who comes to us claims they are "saved," and of course this is something that only God truly knows. People come from different walks of life with different examples of godly people as role models, and simply stating that Jesus is Lord isn't enough. You also have to have Jesus in your heart. Words like trust, hope, faith, and love mean different things to different people, and the simple expression of words isn't enough to know if a man will lead a God-centered life and be easy to work with, or if they simply want to be good and don't know how.

Sometimes men say that they believe *in* God, but when asked if they *believe God*, they don't know the difference. The difference, of course, is that "believing God" is knowing God and "belief in God" is knowing *about* God. Many people know about God, but to truly know someone else requires a whole-hearted desire for a relationship. Becoming an ambassador of heaven requires an awakening of one's spirit and a single-minded desire to please God.

Knowing God is more difficult than knowing anyone else because He is God Almighty, Creator of heaven and earth. How can we possibly know someone who is all-powerful and all-knowing, completely holy, self-existent, and eternal? What do we possibly have in common? I'm sure He's already heard my best jokes hundreds of times, and having an intellectual conversation with me can't be all that interesting. God is the one person with whom I am most unequally yoked.

Knowing another person involves them knowing you, as well as you knowing them. The confiding that I do with my wife, where I talk to her about my dreams and my fears, flows in the opposite direction as she confides in me. As I learn about her struggles with our family, at work, and with our ministry, I participate in her life as she participates in mine. Likewise, knowing God involves Him taking us into His confidence and sharing His thoughts. He invites us to participate in His plans and quickens our spirit so that we can see His presence along the way.

We've witnessed men's hearts being softened, and family members deciding to forget past transgressions as they accept former prisoners back into their lives. I've seen the timing of events that can only be explained by an orchestrated plan. I've become sensitive to what it means to be a brother in Christ to another man, where being in God's family means putting aside my best plans and advice and allowing God to be in charge. I know that calling on the name of Jesus can bring the onslaught of fears to an abrupt halt. And I know that, for some strange reason, God loves me and wants to have a relationship with me.

This insight into what it means to have a relationship with God and that He hears us is something we don't know until we are saved. Many of the men coming to our ministry got into prison because they were chasing sex, money, and drugs. Being in prison doesn't cure those addictions; it just makes them harder to get. Men in prison like to tell stories about what they did in the past and what they plan to do when they get out, and most of these stories have something to do with what got them into prison in the first place.

A man came to our ministry on Tuesday, and by Thursday decided to stay out overnight and break curfew. He came back to the house sometime on Friday in time for our Saturday ministry meeting with the men. Present around the table were about six people in our program, plus my wife, myself, and our house managers. We take turns going around the table by first quoting Scripture, sharing how God has been evident in our lives that week, and plans and support needed for the coming week. Things were going fairly normally until it was the man's turn to speak.

He did not have a Bible verse to share, and when asked about his week he said that he had sinned and had been with a woman (he wasn't married). I said to him and everyone around the table that God wants sex to be between one man and one woman in holy matrimony, and one of the problems of having sex outside of marriage is that it hardens your heart, so that when you do find the right woman it becomes difficult to wait for spiritual side of the relationship to develop before the physical side of the relationship. I'm not sure I was clear when I said that, but the man had his head down and didn't say much. He then raised his head and said that he wasn't with one woman on Thursday night—he was with twelve women. When I heard this, I was caught between giving godly counsel and wondering how that was even possible.

Some men coming into our ministry have had dysfunctional family backgrounds, where prostitution and drug addiction was common. Some had to look out for themselves at an early age because food wasn't always around, and no one cared if they made their bed or did their homework. Growing up in this kind of environment breeds a short-term perspective on life, where learning to hustle and connive are more important than learning to give. Ambassadors of heaven are generally not present in their lives to serve as role models and to provide examples of faith, hope, and love.

When asked on our application if they have experienced "saving faith," the answer these men give is always "yes," but it's not clear what question is being answered, and it could simply mean, "Do you want some help?" When men such as this come out of prison, they often want to go back to their old ways. They have not yet come to Jesus for rest, particularly the younger men who haven't yet developed an urgency to change their lives because they were growing older and time was running out.

There is no "coming back" for individuals who do not have examples of Christian behavior to rely on. For many, there is no "right mind" because there was never anyone to teach them in the first place. The words of the Bible can be just words, without any deep meaning to people not seeking rest in God. What does "love" mean to someone who grew up as a burden and viewed as another mouth to feed? Love is often equated to how someone else makes you feel and doesn't come close to the sacrificial example of Christ, where loving another means to set yourself aside and allow another person to grow. For many men, it's about getting and not giving. It is difficult to give when a person is in a constant state of want, and prison doesn't help alleviate a person's wants.

Men return from prison with much the same mindset that they had when they went into prison. A man who entered when he was eighteen years old often comes out ten or twenty years later with the wants of an eighteen-year-old. Worse yet, they feel that they've lost the years of incarceration and need to make up for lost time. The hustle is more intense, and the timeline to accomplishment is perceived to be even more immediate than normal. And so, some of the men who come to us do not succeed in breaking the prison cycle. They need to go around the mountain one more time, just as the Israelites needed to try again when they were in the wilderness, until they begin to know God and the purpose of their lives.

Knowing God

Knowing God is more
    than just the knowing of His name
We all know things about Him,
    but that isn't quite the same

We know we serve a loving God . . .
    a "Father God" indeed
Who is always there providing us
    with everything we need

But we need to know Him personally . . .
    we need to know His heart
We need to get so close to Him
    we can't be torn apart

Many people claim to know Him . . .
   some confess they don't
Some will *try* to get to know Him . . .
   many others won't

You will have to spend some time with God
   to really get to know Him
We *say* we want to know Him more,
   but then we have to show Him

He's not at all deceived my friends
   (though our fellowman may be)
He knows ahead of time . . .
   He saw Nathaniel under the tree (John 1:48)

He knows us in our sitting . . .
   as well as in our rising (Psalm 139:2)
Anything we do in life,
   He does not find surprising

For God is not at all surprised
   by anything you do
You can't begin to know Him
   as well as He knows you (Galatians 4:9)

So why go back to living life
   without Him . . . as a slave
Confess to Him if you know Him . . .
   every time you misbehave

He wants to see us reaching out
   to help Him with His plan
To preach and teach and try to reach . . .
   to lift our fellow man

Do we know that much about Him . . .
  do we know what He expects?
Do you know Him well enough to hate
  the things that He rejects?

Do you really, really know Him . . .
  do you want to know Him better?
We can, if we will only take
  the time to read His . . . "letter"

Let us try to spend more time with God
  as this year moves along
Let us get to know God better
  so our race will finish strong

We know that Satan's always busy
  throwing us a curve
Let us spurn that devil and get to know
  the Mighty God we serve.

You Must Be Born Again

*Very truly I tell you, no one can see the kingdom of God
unless they are born again.*

(John 3:3)

The sixth chapter of the book of Isaiah tells the story of how the
prophet Isaiah was called into service for God. It begins in much
the same way that everyone is called—by getting a glimpse of
God and realizing how different He is:

In the year that King Uzziah died, I saw the Lord
seated on a throne, high and exalted, and the train of

his robe filled the temple. Above him were seraphs, each with six sings: With two wings they covered their faces, with two they covered their feet, and with two they were flying. And they were calling to one another:

"Holy, holy, holy is the LORD Almighty; the whole earth is full of his glory."

At the sound of their voices the doorposts and thresholds shook and the temple was filled with smoke. (Isaiah 6:1–4)

What a sight—and what a realization that while I am created in God's image, God is nothing like me. We share the ability to love and morally reason, but God is so much more. While we like to think of God, and especially Jesus, as our friend, it is important to remember that God is God. He is nothing like you, and He is nothing like me. He is holy, set apart from His creation, never changing, and pure. He is the Ancient of Days, the Lord of Lords, the beginning and the end. He is our Creator and our sustainer. And sometimes, if we're paying attention, we get a glimpse of Him as Isaiah did.

The first thing that rushes into our minds when we glimpse God is that we are in trouble. We become acutely aware of our sins and transgressions, every one of them. There is nothing that compares to our infinite God who knows our thoughts before we can form them in our mouths. Isaiah felt the same way:

"Woe to me!" I cried. "I am ruined! For I am a man of unclean lips, and I live among a people of unclean lips, and my eyes have seen the King, the LORD Almighty."

> Then one of the seraphim flew to me with a live coal
> in his hand, which he had taken with tongs from the
> altar. With it he touched my mouth and said, "See,
> this has touched your lips; your guilt is taken away
> and your sin atoned for." (Isaiah 6:5–7)

The Bible teaches us that our words reflect the condition of
our heart (Matthew 12:34), and the seraph was purifying Isaiah's heart by touching the coal to his lips. God cleansed Isaiah,
and this cleansing was a gift to him in the same way that Jesus'
death and resurrection are a gift to us. It is through Jesus that
our sins are forgiven so that we may rightly be called His sons.
All that we need to do is to claim this gift—that is, to confess
our sins and declare that Christ is our Lord.

> Then I heard the voice of the Lord saying, "Whom
> shall I send? And who will go for us?"
>
> And I said, "Here am I. Send me!" (Isaiah 6:8)

This last verse holds the key to being called into service for
God. The key is the word "then." It is only after we are convinced that God is the Lord of lords, and only after we confess
and are cleansed, can we hope to be called into His service. Isaiah got a glimpse of God before being purified, but did not hear
God's call until after he was purified.

Seeing God leads us to being certain of our unworthiness,
and the confession of our sins leads us to God's cleansing grace.
Once this happens, we can then hear God as He calls us into service. There will be no running from our appointed tasks when
we realize there is nowhere to go, and no "going the other way"

when we realize there is only one way worth living. Our only response will be "Here am I. Send me!"

Ambassadors of heaven are "all in" for God, and the only way for man to truly represent God is to want to be aligned with Him. This is a supernatural act because it requires us to set aside our own interest for the sake of the kingdom. It requires a supernatural intervention in our lives for us to be able to hear God so that we can be useful to Him.

Men in our houses are required to participate in an interdenominational Bible study that involves more than five hundred men from about one hundred churches in the Columbus area. Then men are assigned to small groups in which they discuss answers to homework questions, attend a lecture, and are given homework questions designed to bring them closer to God. Our goal in making this a required part of our program is that the men need to get used to talking to other men who are Christians but who also come from a different walk of life. Our men are generally blessed by these discussions, and also bless the discussion as the other men hear about examples and perspectives that are not familiar. There are some men, however, who are not yet born again, and so going to Bible study is viewed as a burden and not a joy.

Our men are also encouraged to enroll in a reentry program offered through a local nonprofit organization. The first three weeks of the program are facilitated by a psychologist who helps the men understand some of the emotional aspects of reentry and its relationship to what got them into prison in the first place. Newly released men have been held for a period of time against their will, in close quarters with people who want to do them harm, and have led a regimented life. Many have PTSD-like symptoms and have trouble being calm. Some of them just aren't ready for an introspective look at themselves. They haven't yet found rest in Jesus.

The men who haven't been saved and aren't really pursuing God are difficult for us. There is no set of rules that can fully define the boundaries of appropriate conduct in our houses, and there is always some scheme being hatched to exploit the program. One man found a website with the answers to the Bible study questions and shared them with everyone else in the houses, telling them that it's much easier to just copy down the right answer than struggle with something that is hard to figure out. This, of course, destroys the entire purpose of doing homework in the first place.

Another man asked to borrow the house lawn mower to cut grass to make some money. When the wheels of the lawn mower fell off, the man suggested that we should have purchased a mower of high quality rather than buying it from a discount retailer. We later found out that the wheels fell off because the man towed the lawn mower on a rope as he rode his bike to a bus stop, took it on the bus with him, cut grass across town, and then spent the rest of the afternoon in a bar drinking away the money he had just made. We needed a new "no borrowing the lawn mower" rule on the books after we figured that one out.

The purpose of our houses is to help men deepen their faith and reclaim their lives. Being a Christian in prison is relatively easy because there is time to engage in Bible study and small group discussions. But the learning is often superficial, because the men have a limited set of opportunities available to apply this knowledge. They don't have much money or possessions, and so sacrificing what they have is limited. Words can be soothing, but they can also be cheap, and it isn't until they are out of prison that their Christian walk is really tested. Putting Christ first when there are many competing demands for your time and money is different than when you're in prison, bored and broke.

Our response to having individuals in the ministry houses who are not seeking God is to wait and let them remain unless they become a threat to others or repeatedly break the house rules, such as breaking curfew. The longer they are out of prison the more they want to define their own destiny, which becomes increasingly at odds with the norms of house behavior.

One of the things that we have for men in our program is a forced savings program where they give us 20 percent of their earnings. The earnings are meant to help them transition to their own apartment where they might need a security deposit, or possibly to help them purchase a car. We usually don't let the men withdraw money from their account with us unless they are ready to leave, in which case we pay them their balance when they have packed their bags. The money grows over time, and for men who simply want a cheap place to live and for whom the house rules seem to be increasingly burdensome, the savings account provides the right incentive for them to want to leave. For men interested in spiritual development, the money in the savings account isn't anywhere near the same temptation. Some of our men, who were with us for two years, had saved enough to make a down payment on home or purchase a car. We try to let God be in charge and patiently wait to see what happens. Our ministry houses would drive a person crazy if we didn't believe that God was in charge and active in the ministry.

Come and Ye Be Saved

We all have heard it said before
    the verse is so well known,
"For it's by grace we are saved, through faith
    and not that of our own."

God loves children, all of us
    Although we misbehave,
He's calling out to each of us to
    Come and be ye saved.

Open up your mind and heart
    Receive the Holy Spirit,
Allow God's love to smother you
    There is no need to fear it.

Come, believe, have faith in Christ
    Trust Him at His word,
He'll rescue you from this world of sin
    (as I am sure you've heard).

"Lost in Space," a common term
    You've heard it over the years,
It also means we may be lost
    In the space between our ears.

For there the problems lie within
    The things we can't believe,
Our intellect will interfere
    With truths we should receive.

But God is faithful in His word;
    Give Him more of your time,
And He'll reveal His truths to you
    And upward you will climb.

> He'll place you on the proper path
> A path already paved,
> With all the reasons needed,
> To come and be ye saved.

Repent

Repent, for the kingdom of heaven has come near.

(Matthew 4:17)

We all come to God in different ways. For some of us, it is a mountaintop experience that awakens our spirit and welcomes us into God's kingdom. For others, it is a much slower process. For me, it began with the realization that the Bible could not possibly have been written by man. Sixty-six chapters, forty authors, 1,500 years in the making, and yet just one consistent message of God's glory, creation, and redemptive plan for mankind. The Holy Spirit was there with the apostle Paul, Moses, and all of the prophets, prompting them with the thoughts they were to record for us. The Bible story is the same from Genesis to Revelation, and it was from this realization that I eventually came to believe and declare my faith in Christ.

I know what it is like to work on group projects. Whenever there are more than two or three coauthors it becomes difficult to maintain a single perspective in writing a paper or report. Everyone wants to add their own thoughts, and when this happens the writing loses its focus. But the Bible is flawless in its story—consistent, pointed, and true. Forty authors? Impossible. One author? That's much more believable.

Introspection about God is the first step in developing a Christian walk. If we are to be used as instruments in God's service, to bring about lasting change in this world, we first need to take on the characteristics of Christ. These characteristics are described in the Beatitudes. Blessed are . . .

- the poor in spirit—those who realize that without God they are spiritually bankrupt.

- those who mourn—those who understand the devastation of sin in their lives and their need to return to God.

- the meek—those who wait for God and follow His instruction.

- those who hunger and thirst for righteousness—those who truly want to be right with God.

It is only after we have these in place that we can hope to move on to the remaining blessings described in the Sermon on the Mount, which describe how we should act and treat others.

The most unusual introduction I've ever heard came when I received a phone call at work, and the person on the other end of the line began by saying, "You don't know me from a bar of soap, but. . . ." I had never heard that expression before, and I instantly liked the caller because of his humility. The man went on to say that he was recently released from prison and was staying at an extended-stay hotel for the next week. His sister had put down the money for his week's stay but couldn't offer him a place to stay at her house because of their family situation. He went on to say that he learned about our houses when we were preaching at one of the chapel services about a month before, and he looked me up on the internet.

This man received divorce papers during his last week in prison. He had been given a one-year sentence for a nonviolent crime related to his job at work, where he was the chief operating officer of a small business. No one from his immediate family had visited him or written him a letter during the year he was incarcerated. He came to us in a state of shock, not knowing what to do or where to go. Yet, he desperately wanted to reconnect with his family and be the husband and father that he was before going to prison.

He took a job laying concrete for foundations of houses and businesses. This is tough work that requires a lot of muscle for excavating and the setting of forms for the concrete when it is poured. He was in his mid-fifties and by far the oldest member of the crew and was given the nickname "Tooth" for being "long in the tooth." Driving to and from the worksite with the younger men in a van involved everyone (but him) smoking marijuana and cussing. He would come back to the ministry house at night completely exhausted. During our house meetings on Saturday he could barely move. But he wanted to continue, because the money was good, and he would be able to help his wife and children whom he loved. He would send them money that they needed, but they didn't yet want to fully embrace him.

Despite his attempts to make amends, the divorce papers turned into court dates, and the court date turned into a time to finalize everything. The divorce had driven him to be somewhat depressed, but he didn't give up. He found a church where he felt comfortable and attended regularly, and was single-minded in wanting to restore what he had. The divorce agreement, from my perspective, was very one-sided as it would put him in a state of poverty for the foreseeable future. But he accepted it and had hoped that things would work out.

He continued to hold out hope until the day his divorce was finalized, but the divorce went through anyway. On that day, he told us that he was feeling his lowest, driving an old beat-up truck down the highway, when he received a phone call from a man who would eventually give him the break he needed—helping manage an apartment complex near campus. God's timing was impeccable—as if He had reached down from heaven at exactly the right moment to give our man the reassurance he needed. He dedicated himself to his job, moved out of our ministry houses, and quickly rose to take on bigger and more responsible roles in that organization. His family eventually warmed up to him, and he is currently interacting with his ex-wife and children.

We never know exactly what goes on in the lives of the men who come to us, why people act as they do, and what hurt going to prison caused in others that makes it difficult for them to forgive and move forward. But I know that this man humbled himself and was willing to make himself a doormat because of the guilt he had in his heart. He also had something that he wanted to reclaim—a place to come back to. It sometimes takes a long time to realize a homecoming, but the hope of that future event can sustain a person to work through the heartbreaks and focus on something more important than the choices that currently confront them. In other words, he had a "right mind" to come back to, and was willing to pay the price.

Sin, in whatever form it takes, takes us further away from where we want to go, keeps us longer than we want to stay, and ends up costing more that we want to pay. Knowing God's kingdom is near helps us to continue to move forward.

Consider Your Ways

When things are just not going right
　　And you wish for better days
Consider all the things you do
　　Stop! And—consider your ways

Not long ago I was living
　　In a backsliding condition
Using automatic pilot
　　On the highway to perdition

I knew that I was doing wrong
　　(The truth I tried to fight)
Like many others in the church
　　I wasn't living right

Yes, I knew that I needed help
　　The Spirit made me sure
But still my flesh was in control . . .
　　Crying out for more

I couldn't stop it all alone
　　(I had put God on the shelf)
But He reached down and did for me
　　Things I couldn't do for myself

So lift your eyes unto the hills
　　From whence your help will come
Our help cometh from the Lord
　　And we're all in need of some

The thoughts God has toward me,
    Are good and will not bend
Not of evil . . . not of harm
    To give me a fruitful end

I have sewn much, and brought in little
    I have eaten but not had enough
I drank but was not filled with drink
    What was easy I made to be tough

My clothes, my cars, my home are gone
    But I shouldn't find that odd
I earned wages to put into bags with holes
    Instead of investing in God

I was caught up, struggling, and going through hell
    And wishing for better days
And the Lord spoke through Haggai, saying
    You must consider your ways

How are you when you're out of sight
    And you think the church won't know?
How do you talk, what's on your mind?
    Where are the places you go?

Do you cuss and lie, and lust and deny
    And think that it's okay?
Do you thank our God for everything?
    Or sometimes forget to pray!

For the eyes of the Lord are upon you
    He sees everything you do
There is no shadow or darkness
    No hiding place for you

Because I turned my back on Him
    (And also on my brothers)
He revealed my ways and exposed me
    In the open sight of others

You may not be as bad as some
    You may be living well
But we must allow God to use us
    To help others not to fail

We are ambassadors for Christ
    Giving glory to the Lord
To be confused about that
    We just cannot afford

So wake up if you're living
    In a backsliding condition
It's time to gain an appetite
    For spiritual nutrition

Grow in faith, learn to pray
    Read and absorb your Bible
Believe that Jesus Christ our Lord
    Is totally reliable

When things are just not going right
    And you wish for better days
Perhaps you need to spend some time
    Considering your ways

Discussion Questions

1. Who were people in your life who provided a godly example, so that you could have a right mind?

2. How can you tell that someone has a priority for God in their lives? What kind of screening question would you ask on an application to determine this? What would you watch for?

3. Describe a time in your life that required perseverance.

4. Is there something in your life that you lost and want to reclaim?

5. How would you counsel the man who visited the twelve women?

6. What would you say to a man who was determined to make up for lost time but was using poor judgment?

7. Would you have thrown the man with the lawn mower out of the house? Why or why not?

8. How would you counsel the man whose wife divorced him?

Chapter 2

BE A DISCIPLE

Before accepting Jesus Christ as my personal Savior and Master, I (Timothy) used to attend church just as a nominal Christian. One day I went to my boss's house; he was a very devoted born-again Christian. I hated him mostly just because he used to talk about Jesus. He welcomed me so nicely and prepared tea. Before taking tea, he asked me if we could read the Word of God then take tea. He took the Bible and started reading and expounding scriptures on salvation. Then he came to the end and asked me if I understood what the Bible said to me.

I felt, straight in my heart, something pushing from the inside out of me to repent and receive Christ to be my Savior and Master. He asked me to kneel down, then led me to Christ Jesus. The moment I confessed of my sin, repented, then asked Jesus to enter in me, I felt something like power from above entering my heart and it turned around everything in me. The first thing I noticed was that immediately, a passion to love my boss triggered me powerfully, to the point that I even wanted to know the church he was attending.

In the evening I made sure I followed him as he drove to the church; I was just walking, but making sure I knew where he was headed. He ended up at a school that they used as their church. I entered into that classroom, and we had a very powerful church service. I listened to the praise and worship service, then came the Word of God taught by the pastor of that church, Alfred Mwakitalima. That word sunk deeply in my soul and confirmed in me that I had made the right decision.

The following day as I went to work, I felt a loving passion toward wanting to meet the boss. Remember, this was the person I had hated most and didn't want to see myself being close to, just because he talked about Jesus Christ and wanted us to follow Christ the way he did. God turned that around, in a very miraculous way. From the moment I accepted Jesus to be my Savior and Master, I now wanted to be with this same person almost all the time, just to hear him talk about Jesus Christ.

God changed my heart. Instead of hating salvation, I coddled it; I embraced it tightly. I rejoiced in seeing myself coming back to my senses. From there and then, my heart kept craving for God's presence, God's Word, and for opportunities to serve Him.

According to what have I seen going on in my life since then, I can strongly say that there is truth of spiritual divine salvation that has the ability to change anybody who is willing to give him/herself to Christ Jesus. I have seen it happen to others, and to myself. For forty-three years now (since 1976, the time I accepted Jesus Christ as my personal Savior and Master), I have walked with Christ Jesus and have proven all that is said in the Bible to be true.

What made me to continue enjoying the sweetness and joy in my daily life was that I had made a strong, uncompromising decision to abide in Christ. I don't see how I can think of leaving Jesus. Many times I do say to myself: I wish I could have been like this from my childhood. I wish I had not been derailed by sin. My desire is to continue abiding in Him.

> Being an ambassador requires us to believe in Him, listen to Him, and abide in Him.

Believe in Me

Do not let your hearts be troubled. You believe in God; believe also in me.

(John 14:1)

God is always calling us. He's always inviting us into His house. There's something about His invitation that is intriguing and warming, and when we first begin to notice it, we know that something special is happening. We are lured into His presence by the circumstances He orchestrates in our lives. At first, we don't really understand that it is truly God doing the calling—it just seems to us to be a good thing to do.

I was invited to be on staff at a church summer camp when my children were young. I had never gone to church camp before in my life and had no idea how much fun it would be. It was a week that was both the shortest and the longest I had ever experienced. We would wake up in the morning and go down to the mess hall for breakfast. I didn't have to worry about what to cook, or what to wear. Seven t-shirts and a pair of shorts (plus underwear) was about all I really needed for the week. Activities were planned by someone else, there was a mission trip to go on during the week that involved volunteering at a social service agency, and daily Bible studies. What was remarkable to me about this experience is the positive attitude everyone had. I loved every minute of it, and at the end of the week, when looking back on my experience, I thought it went by too quickly. It was heavenly.

I ended up going back as a staff member at this camp for twelve years. After my kids were long out of the house, I'd spend one week each summer at camp with my counselor friends, many of whom were ministers and youth ministers at their churches. I just loved it. The friendships were real, the time spent apart from the regular world was relaxing, and I enjoyed my work with the campers. I felt that I was being of service to God and useful to the development of children. I didn't know it then, but this was beginning of the greatest one-two punch ever delivered in my life.

During my years on staff I attended Bible studies at my church, but unfortunately my church was not a strong Bible-believing church. We studied the Bible more from a historical perspective than from a perspective of truth. The context surrounding the Bible passages was emphasized most, and through these studies I learned to believe *in* God, but I hadn't yet learned how to *believe God*. The Bible studies were fun; they reminded me of my camp experience, and we usually convened at a local bar for a beer and fellowship after the study. What could be wrong with that?

At a later point in time, I started to attend a serious Bible study—and by serious, I mean one that involved homework and emphasized the central questions, "What do you think God wants you to know in this passage?" and "How is this manifest in your life?" We really studied the Bible and didn't treat it as the opening line in a night of fellowship. I was intrigued, and the warming I experienced at camp was magnified by realizing that the Bible was a gift to us from God. I also saw myself as being steeped in sin. God convicted me that I couldn't remain the person I was. This was punch number two—I had to get away from me!

God reaches us in different way, but the calling is always to Christ. True faith always involves a person's head, heart, and hands. Some come to Christ in a mountaintop experience of emotion, others through a desire to serve, and some through a goal of understanding who God is. In the end, though, all three of these components operate in someone who is living out their faith. One challenge in being a Christian example for someone else is sensing how God is calling to them and meeting them where they are. Christ meets us where we are and works to help us become the people He has designed us to be. We need to meet people where they are, not where we want them to be.

A man came to us from a prison where he got involved with the chapel services. He would read the Bible, but it didn't make sense to him. He was an intelligent person, but the Bible had not yet been revealed to him in a way that he could understand. The nice thing about him is that he would admit his lack of understanding. He didn't reject what he didn't understand; he just didn't understand it.

Many people seeking God take on the worldly perspective that if they cannot understand something, it must not be true. Sometimes they make fun of it, or mock what they don't understand, to make themselves feel better. When studying the Bible, this orientation manifests itself in the central question "What does this say to me?" instead of "What is God trying to *tell* me?" Approaching the Bible with a self-centered point of view leads to superficial questions, rejection of Scripture, and a buffet-style approach to faith where we consume only the spiritual food we already know will taste good.

Wholehearted faith requires us to take on the perspective that we should expect to not fully understand the Bible. If we think about God as the true author of the Bible and the fact that God is infinite, we can't avoid the conclusion that we won't initially understand most of what the Bible says. We have to work at it, chew it over, test it, take it on board, and otherwise see if it is true. We have to move from knowing about Scripture to knowing Scripture, in much the same way that we need to not just know about God but know God. This process can take a long time.

Our man didn't give up. He came to Bible study on Tuesday nights and openly admitted what he didn't understand. The other men around the table would offer their perspectives on the passage, and he got to see that different interpretations of a single Scripture can all be correct. The fact that God speaks to us individually through the Bible is a great relief to men learning to do the right thing, as it encourages them to figure out biblical truths and how it applies to their lives.

The man gradually began to see the truth, and I admire him for sticking with it. I think he was trying to make things more complicated than they needed to be, and when he started from some basic truths (e.g., I am not God, I am a sinner, I need God, God loves me) he was able to deepen his faith and move forward. His brain had gotten in the way of his spiritual development; nonetheless, God broke through and improved his vision because he was willing to learn. One of the first steps in becoming an ambassador is to be willing to learn so that we can teach others about Christ.

Learning . . . Still Learning

When left up to me . . .
    I did many things wrong
I strayed to those places . . .
    I didn't belong

I often did things
    that were not in God's will
Regretting it afterward . . .
    I did them still

I am not the most righteous . . .
    please help me to see
It's not me drawing You, Lord . . .
    it's *You* drawing me

For over the years
    I have held on to doubt
Not truly believing . . .
    I sought to find out

Like Thomas, I had
    to see things for myself
(My "faith by just hearing" . . .
    was up on the shelf)

You are teaching me Lord,
    through experiences past
And I'm learning to trust you . . .
    trust you at last

So many wonders . . .
    I have watched you perform
Astounding, unnatural . . .
    out of the norm

Going before me . . .
    preparing the scene
Keeping me healthy
    and keeping me "clean"

Preparing me blessings,
    before I arrive
You quicken my spirit . . .
    I'm feeling alive

I am blessed in my Spirit;
    I am blessed in my seed
I am blessed in all places
    whenever there's need

The blessings you give . . .
    that I'm bound to receive
Are impacting my faith . . .
    as I come to believe

I have learned not to trust
    everything that I've heard
Unless it's supported
    by what's in Your word

The Bible is fact . . .
    it's been tested and tried
For there is the truth
    that cannot be denied

If we take time to read it . . .
>   again and again
We will learn to believe
>   that our God is our friend

Keep drawing me nearer,
>   Lord . . . nearer to thee
Help me to *learn*
>   how You want me to be

I want to be close to You . . .
>   Much closer yet
And the more time we spend . . .
>   the closer we get

And I'm getting to know You
>   more . . . each passing day
Believing by faith . . .
>   in all that you say

I am learning, still learning
>   to trust in you more
Please teach me those things
>   I did not learn before.

Listen to Me

Again Jesus called the crowd to him and said, "Listen to me, everyone, and understand this."

(Mark 7:14)

Before I (Benjamin) was arrested for the very last time (the arrest that landed me in prison), I was absolutely certain that God was

speaking to me telling me to *stop* what I was doing. No, it wasn't
an audible voice, but it may as well have been. The signs were
so obvious and consistent, so timely and unique, that it was
eerie—or better put, supernatural?

Two weeks before that arrest I kept seeing police cruisers
with someone handcuffed in the back seat (as I had been so
many times before). Of course it's natural to see people in the
back seat of a cruiser because people get arrested every day, but
I didn't normally *see* it every day . . . several times. It's not like I
lived right next to the police station.

In front of my house, behind my house, up the street from
my house, at the supermarket, in front of the temp service (my
employer), and everywhere else I went I would see the same
event: someone handcuffed in the back of a cruiser. I was never
able to make out who was being arrested, but I knew these were
warning signs for me.

On Sunday, February 3, 2008, I was at a friend's house not
far from mine . . . doing my thing. Another friend came in, and
when he saw me, he said, "Man, I thought you got busted. . . .
I just saw the police putting someone in the back of a cruiser in
front of your house and I thought it was you!" Talk about things
that make you go hmmm!

I pondered over that for about an hour then decided to
leave, even though I had only made about $40 cash and a bottle
of pills that I could have resold for another $40. I thought I
should take my fifth of liquor, my bag of weed, my bottle of
pills, and my quarter ounce of crack that I had just bought, go
home and shut down for the night.

This was the first time anyone else had mentioned what I
had been seeing so regularly. I could feel it on the inside that
this was my final warning. Since no one knew that I had the

quarter-ounce (you never tell crack addicts you have that much crack unless you know they have that much money), I told them that I was going to "re-up." My lady friend and I left, but we never made it to my house. We got about fifty feet from my backyard gate and a cruiser rolled up on us. It was 1:15 a.m. Monday morning; and by 1:30 a.m. on February 4, 2008, I was sitting handcuffed in the back of a cruiser. I could hear a voice inside saying, "I tried to warn you, but you would not acknowledge me—rather, you acted like you didn't hear me."

I thought to myself, *That's what you get, Benjamin! Now you're on your way to prison because you wouldn't pay attention to the warning signs, which were God's voice speaking loud and clear. That's what you get—undesirable consequences.* Then I began thinking about all the previous times I had failed to acknowledge God's voice. This was nothing new to me. I was in the habit of ignoring the voice of God as if it didn't matter what He said. I was in the habit of doing what I wanted to do, when I knew for certain it was not of God. Have you ever been there?

Many of us will ask, "How do I know when I am hearing the voice of God?" Well, we must learn to test the words we are hearing. Job 12:11 says, "Does not the ear test words as the tongue tastes food?" If it doesn't sound like something God would say, it's probably not His voice. He is always telling us to do the right thing, the best thing, that which will benefit the kingdom instead of ourselves. Our enemy is always telling us to do that which will bring us self-satisfaction, however temporary. We like self-satisfaction, don't we? We may not want to hear the voice of God interrupting our self-satisfying ways.

We may not hear or admit to hearing God's voice because we know we've done something wrong, or because we don't want to change. We know that God is always asking us to change. He is always asking us to give up something that we would like to keep, specifically our will . . . our self.

Do we sometimes hide when we hear God's voice because we are afraid? Or do we pretend not to hear Him because we don't want to hear Him say *stop* what we don't want to stop doing? Is it really that hard to hear God's voice, or is our own voice so loud it drowns His out?

Two Voices

There are two voices in my head
    I call both of them "Something Said"
They both tell me what I should do
    I must decide between the two

If I don't like the end result
    I must accept that it's my fault
So I must learn to stop! And think!
    From which one's cup do I choose to drink?

I must stop denying all along
    That I have preferred to do what's wrong
For even when I disagreed
    I done things that brought harm . . . to me

God knew whom Jonah's words would reach
    That's why He told him to go and preach
But Jonah heard the other voice
    And thereby made another choice

Some of us will do the same
    When Something Said call us by name
One tells us to do what's right
    The other one then wants to fight

Something Said, "I need a drink."
    Something Said, "No! Stop and think."
Something Said, "Let's drink one beer,
    and then we'll stop . . . have no fear!"

Something Said, "One is too many;
    think again, and don't have any."
One Something Said will keep you sane
    The other one will cause you pain

Which "Something Said" should I listen to?
    They both are telling me what to do
Something said, "I'm really tired;
    can I miss work and not get fired?"

Something Said, "Don't be a jerk;
    just get up and go to work."
Something Said, "Just tell a lie;
    your dog is sick . . . about to die."

"You had a flat . . . the car wouldn't start;
    they'll believe you if you tell it smart."
Something said, "Just keep it real;
    you know how lying makes you feel."

You're driving down a busy street
>   To meet someone you need to meet
And someone cuts in front of you
>   What is it that you think to do?

Something Said to scream and shout
>   Pull beside them and cuss them out
Something Said, "That's not the way;
>   that's not who you are today."

Which something should we listen to?
>   They both tell us what we should do
One of them deserves a toast
>   The other one has hurt us most

Something Said, "If you're discrete;
>   it's okay to sneak and cheat.
Variety is the spice of life. . . .
>   So what if we're man and wife?"

Something Said, "Are you insane?
>   The Bible makes it very plain.
Once you choose to say, 'I do,'
>   it's you and her or him and you."

Something Said, "Well, I'm still single;
>   it's okay to mix and mingle,
as long as I watch out for tricks . . .
>   and don't get caught up in the mix."

Something Said, "You might be right,
    but watch the things you do at night.
Remember Joseph had to—*run*
    to keep from giving in to—*fun*."

There are two voices in my head
    One wants me to live, one wants me dead
And all day long I hear their voice
    But it's up to me to make that choice

One full of love . . . one full of sin
    And they always fight to see who'll win
Which Something Said should we listen to?
    They both tell us what we should do

Well, think real hard and you can tell
    One is from God . . . the other is from hell

Something told me that!

Abide in Me

*Remain in me, as I also remain in you. No branch can
bear fruit by itself; it must remain in the vine. Neither
can you bear fruit unless you remain in me.*

(John 15:4)

A couple of years ago my (Greg) car had a short in the electrical
system. I could tell because my electric odometer would flicker
sometimes, and my car wouldn't accelerate properly. I took it

into the local repair shop to do some tests on the electrical system, but they said it was fine. I knew that it wasn't but didn't want to spend the money to take it into the dealer, which I thought would end up costing a lot of money. I decided to ignore the problem and see what would happen.

I had driven from Columbus to Cincinnati for business, where the car died in the parking lot of a store. I was lucky that it didn't die on the interstate. The store had an auto repair department, but they couldn't find the problem either. There was an automobile dealer down the road that could take a look at it and I had it towed to them. By the end of the day they diagnosed that the battery had an electrical short. Once a car is disconnected from the battery, the entire car shuts down and is unresponsive.

I think the most bone-chilling passage in the Bible appears in Romans 1:18–31, where Paul describes what happens when we disconnect ourselves from God. God's wrath against mankind is revealed as man refuses to acknowledge Him and live according to the precepts of the Bible. The effect of God's wrath takes place in stages. In the first stage, man's thinking becomes *darkened*:

> Although they claimed to be wise, they became fools and exchanged the glory of the immortal God for images made to look like mortal man and birds and animals and reptiles. (Romans 1:22–23)

While most of us don't overtly worship birds, animals, and reptiles like the ancient Egyptians, we certainly worship wealth, power, fame, and ourselves. I am amazed how much of our time, thoughts, and money we devote to looking good, dressing good, and having power. And for what? There is nothing that lasts in this world except the work we do for Christ (Matthew 6:19–20).

The second stage of our downward spiral comes with sexual impurity and a *degrading* of our bodies:

> Because of this, God gave them over to shameful lusts. Even their women exchanged natural relations for unnatural ones. In the same way the men also abandoned natural relations with women and were inflamed with lust for one another. Men committed shameful acts with other men, and received in themselves the due penalty for their error. (Romans 1:26–27)

The lack of God in our lives leads to the pursuit of greater and greater pleasure because we are never satisfied with what we have. Even worse:

> Having lost all sensitivity, they have given themselves over to sensuality so as to indulge in every kind of impurity, and they are full of greed. (Ephesians 4:19)

I know that God wants His ambassadors to have a soft heart so that we can stand next to our brothers and sisters in Christ and help bear their burdens. Our ability to love another is directly related to the work of the Holy Spirit in our lives. Breaking out of our natural desire to please ourselves is a supernatural act. This passage reminds me of the effects of addiction—wanting to continually feed the habit.

The third and final stage of God's wrath on us is when our thinking becomes *debased* and our thoughts of God are *depraved*. We start calling right wrong, and wrong right:

> Although they know God's righteous decree that those who do such things deserve death, they not only continue to do these very things but also approve of those who practice them. (Romans 1:32)

It's easy to come up with examples of this in our world today when, as a society, we move away from God. I am reminded of a quote by C. S. Lewis, the famous Christian author (*Mere Christianity*, The Chronicles of Narnia), who said, "There are two kinds of people: those who say to God, 'Thy will be done,' and those to whom God says, in the end, 'Thy will be done.'"

It's also easy to see the foolishness of ignoring God and the downward spiral that comes with it in anyone's life. The amazing thing is that we can't see it in ourselves, as we disconnect from God. We're like a car before the battery is completely disconnected—sputtering and under-performing because we don't think much about Him, don't thank Him, and don't spend time with Him. Sometimes this will last for weeks. We start worshipping ourselves, start replacing sensitivity with sensuality, and start justifying our own behavior. And then, by the grace of God, we're pulled back onto the path where right thinking prevails; and we thank God, the creator of the universe, for bothering to take notice of our condition and saving us from ourselves.

Abiding in Christ brings a sense of spiritual fullness that allows you to contend with the world; if problems come your

way, then there is a reason for it that you may not yet understand. Not abiding in Christ leads to an emptiness that needs
to be continuously filled. One path involves discipleship and
the other resembles a free-for-all. Men coming to our ministry
houses sometimes say that they are interested in mentoring others, but what this usually means is that they want someone to
listen to them. Often, they aren't too interested in learning or
sacrificing.

One man who came to us was known as a "yard pastor" in
prison, where he would hold Bible studies and counsel other
inmates. Yard pastors are often problematic because they gain
notoriety by preaching against the prison chaplain, offering a
different point of view (e.g., you'll find heaven in your heart).
We didn't learn about the yard-pastor status of this individual
until he came to us, but he was constantly trying to distinguish
himself at our Bible studies by bringing the discussion to a different Scripture and not giving a heartfelt response to the question being discussed. This individual quickly found a soulmate
after getting out of prison and she listed him as her fiancé on
her church's website (she was a recently ordained minister in a
mainline denomination). He was attracted to her, I think in
part, because he was pressuring his ex-wife into reconciliation at
a time when she wanted to take it slow. Not abiding in Christ
leads to our own set of rules and standards, as opposed to God's
rules and standards.

Men coming into our houses don't pay any rent. They are
literally guests in our houses. We also have an open-refrigerator
policy at one of the houses, where men are encouraged to grab
something from the fridge when they are hungry. We help the
men apply for food stamps when they get out and ask that they
contribute half of their food stamps to the house to buy food for

everyone. We provide a safe place to live and help them take care of their physical needs so that they can grow spiritually. All men express gratitude when they first come to us, especially when they come right out of prison where the food is bad and there is little respect for one another. For many men, this gratitude lasts for about two weeks, until they become accustomed to their surroundings.

One man at the house started to resent the fact that another man would drink his flavored water that he kept in a container in the refrigerator. The product cost about twenty-five cents per pack at the grocery store. The man threatened the other man with bodily harm if he continued to "steal" his drink, and even went as far as to say that he'd put something bad in it so that it would make him sick. I couldn't believe what I was hearing. This man was given a place to stay, a bed to sleep in, and food to eat, but couldn't live with someone drinking his drink. I asked this man to come to his senses. He just couldn't get his mind around the idea of someone taking something from him without asking. I suggested that he might solve this problem once he bought himself his own refrigerator. After experiencing this, I wondered how God puts up with us flavoring His water and then calling it ours.

One of the debates we have from time to time in our ministry is whether a person can lose their salvation. I think that a more tangible question is, "Why do people stop being disciples and stop abiding in Christ?" We can't know whether God has truly touched a man's heart or not at some time in his life, whether they've mistaken a spiritual moment with being born again, or whether their work is motivated by their ego or a sense of altruism. That's God's business, not ours.

What we care about is that they are deepening their spiritual walk with God along the path described by the Bible. Are they understanding the difference between common sense and faith? Are they yielding to God's will and, even better, embracing it? How do they account for events in their lives? The answers to these questions provide an indication of where they are in their spiritual walk. The TV shows they watch, the radio stations they tune into, and what catches their eye as they drive down the street are tangible expressions of their walk with God. Our job in the embassy house is to be patient and let God's work be done in God's time.

Why Don't We Stay Connected?

Getting in touch with God
    is something all of us have "selected"
But isn't it strange how Christians wait
    so long to *stay* connected
We go to church, we read our Bibles,
    we show love and we pray
But all too often we let
    our *strong* connections "slip away"

Our connections to the spirit realm,
    our connections to our God
Our connections to our faith
    that unbelievers find so odd
Satan knows that we're vulnerable
    when we don't remain "plugged in"
And when we are disconnected . . .
    he will lead us into sin

How are *your* "connections" . . .
       are you sure they're tight and strong?
Are you able to tell the devil this:
       "It's best you move along!"?
Can you stand up to his "lures"
       that may be causing you to fuss
Or to bicker or pass judgment,
       or to argue, lie and . . . cuss?

Don't think that you're alone,
       for many "Christians" do these things
When we get disconnected . . .
       this is what the devil brings
Conflict, disagreements . . .
       lack of honesty, and discord
Selfishness, unforgiveness . . .
       things that Christians can't afford

Why do we keep doing this
       and think that it's okay?
Why do we "pull the plug" on God . . .
       and start to drift away?
Even though we are anchored
       so we cannot drift too far
All of us should be
       a little closer than we are

We tend to "*step into the flesh*" . . .
       all of us, every now and then
We've all done this before . . .
       and we'll all do it again
It only takes a second

for our "minds" to disconnect
We "short out" momentarily . . .
    and suffer the effect

Why don't we stay connected
    through the night and all the day?
Once we get connected friends,
    why can't we stay that way?
Because then we would be perfect . . .
    and the chance for that is "slim"
For once we near perfection . . .
    we think we don't need "Him."

Discussion Questions

1. When did you decide to take the Bible seriously?

2. What in the Bible do you have trouble accepting?

3. Can you point to parts of the Bible that seem inconsistent to you? What are they?

4. Recall a time when you ignored the good voice in your head and followed the other voice instead.

5. How do you stay plugged in to God?

6. How would you contend with a "yard pastor"? Do you sometimes preach against others? Why?

7. How would you minister to a person who wants their own flavored drink? What is the flavored water in your life?

8. What would it take for you to have gone into ministry with Benjamin Graham and open up a transition house? How would you know it's the right thing to do?

Chapter 3

BE A SERVANT

There is another level that is very interesting—a level that continues to immerse someone in Christ Jesus. A level that grooms a person toward becoming a strong believer, a strong disciple—a level that gives an indicator of whether or not a person has really made a decision to follow Jesus Christ.

One businessman in our (Timothy's) region, a road contractor, used to collude with government officials to defraud government money. A check for millions of shillings (thousands of dollars in US money) would be prepared to pay the contractor, without even having worked anywhere; that used to be the method the officials and that contractor would use to get money illegally.

One day the contractor was talking a walk near a football stadium, and in that stadium there was a crusade meeting going on. He decided to go, just to watch what was going on. While standing there, the word of God caught him so powerfully that he went forward to the platform to repent of his sins and accept Jesus Christ to be his Savior and Master. Miraculously, that was his turning point from evil to holiness, from the devil to Christ Jesus.

After the crusade, he went straight to one of the churches in the town and continued in prayers of confession, asking for cleansing by the precious blood of Jesus Christ. From there, he went back home. As he was taking his dinner, his friends came in to inform him of the check for 35 million Tanzanian shillings (more than $15,000) that they had prepared for him to pick up tomorrow at the payment master's office.

The guy, without even selecting the words, went straight to the words, "I am now saved. I can't do such a sin as that; I can't steal. I am a born-again Christian, a follower of Jesus Christ, a holy person, and a son of God."

With all those words, his friends asked him, "So do you want to put us at risk? How will we reverse the check if you don't collect it?"

The man just answered them, "I don't know how you will do it; what I know is that I am saved. I can't steal." They left him and went out.

His business was shaken up, and many of his friends left him, but he decided to stand with Christ. God saw his faithfulness and blessed him so abundantly. His business picked up again, and he began working with faithful people. Before his death, he constructed a very big church building that is still being used in Tarime district. Many of his relatives and friends came to Christ through his testimony. His wife is still doing well at the church and is also a chairlady of women's fellowship there. She also does well with her hardware business.

In our previous chapters we talked about the witchdoctor in Raranya. During the course of writing this book, he gave himself to God—to a point where now he is one of the Sunday School teachers in the same church where I preached last year during Easter service, which helped draw him to Christ.

Following Jesus, one has to deny him/herself as the contractor did. Denying oneself is an indication of how much one has decided to follow Jesus. Jesus Himself loved us to a point of giving His life because we were sinners. In other words, His love to us preceded the value of His life. He counted His life as nothing compared to loving us.

> Ambassadors deny themselves and love God.

Take Up Your Cross

> *Then Jesus said to his disciples, "Whoever wants to be*
> *my disciple must deny themselves and take up their*
> *cross and follow me. For whoever wants to save their*
> *life will lose it, but whoever loses their life for*
> *me will find it."*
>
> (Matthew 16:24–25)

The apostle Paul started his letter to the Romans with a declaration of who he was:

> Paul, a servant of Christ Jesus, called to be an apostle
> and set apart for the gospel of God . . . (Romans 1:1)

Paul wasn't interested in his standing within some community or in getting respect from others. He knew that his purpose of life was one thing—to preach about the redemptive work of Jesus Christ on the cross. The reality of redemption was at the forefront of Paul's ministry to the Gentiles. He couldn't forget who he was when he was blinded on the road to Damascus, and he couldn't forget the man he had become because of the grace of God.

Our purpose in life is similar. We are called to witness the power and glory of God, and to rest in knowing that He is working on our behalf in all things. Focusing on the effects of redemption instead of the act of redemption leads to frustration and discouragement. We can't will ourselves to be good, to be kind, or to love. These are outcomes, or signs, of our redeemed state and not the cause of our redeemed state. The source of our redemption is Christ's work on the cross and nothing else.

There was a time in my life that my (Greg's) marriage was about to fall apart. My wife and I had gotten to a point of stalemate, where our interactions would often end in arguments about how the other wasn't being a good husband or wife. It was a stressful time, with both of us working on our careers and having young children to care for. I was mad at my wife for not being there for me, and she was mad at me for being too demanding. I felt that I had fallen to last place in the family priority list and was often not even on the list of things that needed attention. I was miserable, mad, and doing my best to rationalize my actions and arguments. I was hurting and at the time I was sure that it wasn't my fault.

My wife came to the Lord before I did, and I remember when I began to notice a change in her. She didn't want to argue any more, but without an "I'm going to ignore you" attitude. She was calmer and started to say unkind things less.

Then one day, she said something to me that was encouraging. When I was saying something about a struggle at work, and explaining my frustration to her, she said something like "That must be hard for you," and touched my hand when she said it. I was floored and didn't know what to say. Tears came to my eyes, and I knew at that instant that she still loved me.

I think two things happened that turned our marriage around. First, my wife came to Jesus and was redeemed by Him. She became a child of God and drew her strength from Him rather than from me or others around her. She did this quietly, without any announcement. It happened on the day she realized she wasn't going to, or couldn't, change things around her and came to God in submission. She was redeemed from her bondage in the world and bound herself to Christ.

The second thing that happened was that the act of redemption changed how she acted and what she believed. She became kinder, calmer, and more stable. I noticed the change, and I liked what I saw. I wanted some of it, and I enrolled in the same Bible study as her. Soon after, I was also redeemed and gave my life to Christ. The whole process, from her redemption to mine, took about two years. Today, I am so thankful to God for saving us and our marriage.

I was attracted to how my wife set herself apart for the gospel of God. I saw her studying the Bible, doing her homework questions diligently, and trying to derive deep meaning from Scripture. She didn't set out to be more holy, but it was her personal holiness that drew me to her and to God. It was only through loving God with all of her heart, with all of her soul, and with all of her mind that she was able to love me from the overflow of God's love back to her (Matthew 22:36–40).

> Very truly I tell you, unless a kernel of wheat falls to the ground and dies, it remains only a single seed. But if it dies, it produces many seeds. (John 12:24)

Our purpose is to live redeemed lives, by dying to ourselves and living in great thankfulness for what Christ has done on the cross. Others will see the change in us and will be drawn to Christ. We share the gospel by giving thanks to God.

A man came to our ministry after serving the second of two sentences for child endangerment. It was the second time he had engaged in behavior that threatened his children, and he had anger issues. His second sentence put him in prison for three years, and he was anxious to reconnect with his wife and four children.

The day he came to us he got the news from the parole board that he would not be allowed to have contact with his children for at least a year. I remember seeing him that evening in the sanctuary of the church hosting the Bible study. We would start the night off singing a couple of hymns before breaking off for our small-group discussion, and he was sitting in a pew with his head down, crying. I went up to him to ask if he was OK, and he just shook his head. "They won't let me see my children," he said. "I can't see my kids." It was a devastating time for him when he learned that even though he knew was ready, the state of Ohio wasn't ready to trust him with his children.

This man had to work through the guilt and the shame of his past behavior. He, more than anyone we've had in the houses, had to learn to deny himself and move forward. He had to learn to be content with what he had (Philippians 4:11–13). It wasn't what he wanted, but he knew that if he remained faithful to the mandate of the parole board he would eventually be reconciled to his children.

Learning to be content is the key to servanthood, because it allows us to focus our energy for God's purposes rather than wasting time "probing the wall." Many of the men who come to us want to test the boundaries of the house rule and see what they can get away with. The expression "nobody told me that" is the hallmark of someone trying to get the most while doing the least. For some of the men, probing the wall seems like a natural behavior after years of incarceration. For others, it's just good sport.

We have an in-house Bible study every Tuesday night where I barbeque some food and we have dinner before discussing a Scripture passage. I usually make chicken that I marinate in Italian salad dressing, along with some hot dogs, potato salad, and dessert. The guys love my chicken (or so they say) because it's tender and I suspect the chicken in prison is anything but tender. We pray and then go into the dining room at Fort Jackson for dinner. The dining room is large enough to hold about twenty men, including the chairs around the table which can hold ten men.

The men can take all the food they want and we never run out, but every once in a while we get a man in the house who quickly finishes his first plate of food and then sneaks back into the kitchen to take some of the chicken and dessert for his lunch later in the week. The problem is that he will do this before everyone is done eating, and some of the guys go back in for seconds because they are still hungry. When I point out that they shouldn't take food for future meals until everyone is done with the current meal, some of the men just can't understand why that would be the fair thing to do.

My goal is to have everyone eat their fill, and then to split the food equally across men in our two houses for lunches if someone wants a to-go bag. The problem with rushing back into the kitchen is that the person doing this is taking a disproportionate amount for himself.

It doesn't just stop with the food. This sort of behavior—taking as much as you can and giving as little as you can—shows up in other ways, including doing work (e.g., cleaning up) around the house.

Some men never really engage in the ministry and the community we try to foster. Their eyes and hearts are on something else. They are not content with where they are and "kick" against the system. Once the man described above accepted the fact that it would be a year before he could see his children, he unpacked his bags, settled in, and began being a servant of God. He took interest in the other men in the houses and became an asset to the ministry. His focus was no longer on himself, but on God.

How Can I Serve You Today?

Help me, dear Lord, to find my purpose
I really don't know where to start

Open the eyes of my mind and my spirit
And open the eyes of my heart

My purpose eludes me . . . of this I am sure
If my selfishness lives at my side

Alter my stubbornness, clean up my will
And please, Lord, cancel my pride

Grant me direction through reading your Word
For I know my assignment is there

Contained in the Scriptures my purpose is clear
If I study and read them with care

Help me to see you wherever I go
With continuing focus on You

Lead me and guide me and teach me, dear Lord
To do as you want me to do

Which way should I go, to whom should I speak?
Who is it that I am to see?

Abolish my blindness so I can discern
The steps you have ordered for me

What would you have me to do, dear God?
What would you have me to say?

Reveal my purpose and cause me to know
How I can serve you today?

Love God

Love the Lord your God with all your heart and with
all your soul and with all your mind and with
all your strength.

(Mark 12:30)

The life of every Christian is marked by the critical decision of deciding whom to follow. Do we follow Christ as our Lord and Savior, or do we try to follow a middle ground where we manage our relationship with God? I've heard some people talk about how they manage their time with God. They feel the need to come back to God if they are away from Him after being preoccupied by worldly events. Others, particularly those new to faith, feel they can run off and "visit" sin without it affecting them much. The truth is that none of us are strong enough to resist temptation without God's help. Visiting sin includes all those things that used to get us into trouble, including running around with some of our old friends. The key, some feel, is that everything is returned to being right once we manage our way back to God.

The concept of managing our relationship with God is a silly one. Isaiah, speaking to the Jewish nation, describes God in a series of comparisons as he writes:

> Who has measured the waters in the hollow of his hand, or with the breadth of his hand marked off the heavens? Who has held the dust of the earth in a basket, or weighed the mountains on the scales and the hills in a balance? Who has understood the mind of the LORD, or instructed him as his counselor? Whom did the LORD consult to enlighten him, and who taught him the right way? Who was it that taught him knowledge or showed him the path of understanding? (Isaiah 40:12–14, NIV1984)

The answer is "God alone." Have you ever stood on the coast and looked out over the ocean? Have you ever stood on top of a mountain and surveyed the heavens? Creation pales in comparison to God. Has anyone tried to gauge the mind of the Lord? Do you think that God is ever confused or surprised? Can you imagine Him saying, "I am completely at a loss—will you help me on this problem?" Of course not.

How then can we possibly manage our relationship with God? How do we manage our way back to the God of the universe, the Creator of all, who is all-knowing and all-powerful? The God who knew us before we were born and who knows each of us by name? The God who carries us close to His heart? How do we manage our relationship with the God who loves us so much that He sent His own Son to die for our sins? The answer is: we can't.

As we consider the choices we face each day—our choice of friends, our choice of activities, our choice of what deserves our attention—we must consider God. We must consider what He thinks of our choices, knowing He is there with us as we make those choices. Deep in our hearts we know that God has better plans for each of us than we have for ourselves. Choose to love Him enough so you can see how big He really is.

Being wholeheartedly committed to God is something that all of us fail at. There just isn't any way I can pray all of my waking hours or hold captive every thought that comes into my head. My mind wanders, and the battle between my spirit and my flesh is something that is always present. It is sometimes difficult to remember to pick my head up and see the battle before me, and to be in it but not be part of it. Ambassadorship is difficult because we live in a foreign land and we don't always remember that our citizenship is elsewhere.

Men coming to our program belong to all sorts of other "countries." The most prevalent is the land of "me, mine, and myself." One night at our in-house Bible study, one of the men expressed a thought that was counter to the teachings in the Bible. I don't remember exactly what was said, but I remember the room going silent as everyone waited to see what was going to be said next. Since I was leading the study, I asked the man if he could point to a passage in the Bible that would support what he was saying. He said that he couldn't, but what he expressed was just how he was feeling.

The house manager of Fort Jackson at the time was a large man who could have easily played NFL football if it hadn't been for a heroin addiction that sidelined his college playing. When you shake his hand, your hand literally becomes engulfed in a mass of flesh and the only hope of retrieving it is to go in with a strong handshake—anything less leaves your fingers twisted up.

The house manager looked the man in the eye and said two things. The first thing he said is that this was a Bible study, not a knitting party—that we all have feelings, but that our goal tonight was to study the Bible and understand what *God* was trying to say to *us*. The second thing he said was that his feelings are what got him into prison in the first place, and that our hearts are deceitful above all things (Jeremiah 17:9). As I heard this, I remember thinking that it was nice to be part of a men's ministry where you don't always have to pussyfoot around sensitive issues.

When a man receives a response like this, they react in two ways—they either appreciate the frankness of what was said and acknowledge their faulty thinking, or they are offended that someone would speak to them in this way. People from the land of "me, mine, and myself" will be offended because they are not ready to change and don't want to be edified. There is no iron sharpening iron (Proverbs 27:17) in that land.

The man who uttered the words about his feelings left the ministry house within a week and went back to his drinking and homelessness. About a year later he showed up at a church where we served on Sunday morning, looking for some clothes and breakfast. We reconnected with him and gave him some money for food after he gave us an academy performance about his regret about leaving, his family whom he doesn't often see, and his need for a new pair of shoes.

He later came back to us when he was being discharged from the hospital after a cardiac scare, when they had to put in a pacemaker. He didn't have anywhere else to go, so he gave the discharge person at the hospital our address. He swore that he was ready to turn his life around this time, but he went back to drinking when he started to feel better. He just didn't want to, or couldn't, change. Just recently, however, he enrolled in an addiction counseling program and showed up at our house meeting a changed man. He is standing with God again and we pray that it continues.

There are many men like this who we are unsuccessful at "reaching" and seeing a change in their lives. We know that our ministry is made up of people who love God and want to do good, but we're not really prepared to provide psychological help for someone who has mental health issues. All that we really do is provide a safe environment for men who want to pursue God; we end up referring men to other treatment facilities but can't be sure they are following up on their appointments. Many of the men come back to us at some later time, either because of the good chicken on Tuesday nights or, more realistically, because they've experienced God in some way while they were with us.

When we are asked how many of the men that come to us have a successful outcome, our response is "100 percent." We do our best to show the love of Christ to all the men and I think we're successful in doing this. We aren't in charge of the harvest, and for a lot of men in our program we are only seed planters. Our recidivism rate is about 20 percent, which is well below the state average, but the men who come to us are generally very interested in improving themselves in the first place and so a simple comparison to the state average isn't really fair. Our real hope rests with God, who knows that it is our intent to serve Him.

It's Something We Must Do

We're changing from our former ways,
    to leave them in the past
No more living in the darkness . . .
    the lights came on at last

We're seeing things more clearly now,
    we understand what's true
We know without a doubt,
    this is what God wants us to do

To rise up from our falling down,
    and step up to the plate
To become a man of principles . . .
    and *no*! It's not too late

There's still some sin within us,
    but the God in us is greater
Let's tell our friends who will not change,
    "I'll have to catch you later"

I have to separate myself
    from things I do no more
You're welcome to come in,
    but I will have to close this door

God had to do some work on me
    to get me back on track
So I'm not taking chances,
    for I won't be falling back

We have to take a *stand*, my friends,
    against that evil day
We can't go back to living life
    the same old way

It doesn't take a lot of thought
    to know that this is true
But we can't just think about it . . .
    It's something we must do

Discussion Questions

1. What daily bread or chicken do you take so that you're sure you have some for later?

2. Have you unpacked your bags, or are you looking to move on in your life?

3. In what part of your spiritual walk do you hedge your bets? Do you tithe? Do you serve the poor and visit the widow? Why not?

4. How do you react to sharp criticism? Do you find yourself thinking, "I don't mind the fact that he said it, but I'm offended by how he said it"?

5. How do you, or would you, measure success in your service to others?

6. How would you teach someone to be a servant? Serve who? How much? In what way? Are boundaries needed? What might be good boundaries?

7. How would you help someone to learn to be content?

8. Are there people in your life whom you just haven't reached yet? Who are they?

Chapter 4

BE TRUSTING

What I (Timothy) have learned in walking with Christ is that faith in Christ is the leading factor. I had to learn to depend on Christ in everything I do, and I have seen the benefit of that. Before coming to Christ, I was doing everything on my own; I didn't know it was God who was orchestrating my life but depended on myself. Today, every time I reflect back to the days I walked without Jesus, I see many wrong things that I did and ask myself, "How could I do that?" or "Why did I have to do that?" When I relate my former life (before coming to Christ) with the story of the prodigal son, I feel similar.

I thank God that it was not by works and deeds that made Him save me but that I am justified by faith in Christ. I feel being connected to Him, I am an ambassador of heaven here on Earth. This is because God justified me by faith in Christ. My job since I gave my life to Christ is to ensure I cling on Him. I am bonded, I am glued, I am fused in Christ.

This is what my heart yearns to do for the impoverished children of Raranya. God assigned me to start a school and enroll the children who come from destitute families, families that don't even know Christ. The goal of the Leaders School is to groom these orphan children to a level of being saturated in Christ, and to have high-quality education that will enable them to become world-changers, starting with their guardians/parents, the Raranya community, and beyond.

The love of God always seeks to transform those who come to Him. One sex worker by the name Anna at Singida came to an evangelistic meeting, and by God's grace gave her life to Christ. As she went on the platform to give her testimony of what happened to her, people could not believe what she was saying. I remember hearing her say, "You will see me." Her life was transformed to a point that she made many others come to Christ. At first people could not believe she had changed, especially married people; but as time went by, they accepted what she said at the platform: "You will see me." She was changed; she was another new person in the same body.

Her lifestyle was changed from hanging out in bars and dancing; she was tied up with church services and joined a church choir. Every time their choir was ministering somewhere, a crowd of people would go just to see her ministering in the choir. She became a talk of the town.

Always her words were, "Jesus has done a great thing to me, enabling me to come out of sex slavery. I was a slave of sex, I was selling myself to men every day, gaining nothing but Satan's deception, humiliating myself and my parents, my relatives, my friends. But now I am free; I am proud of being myself and that I am serving God through singing."

> Ambassadors are justified and transformed
> by faith in Christ.

Be Justified by Faith in Christ

Not everyone who says to me, "Lord, Lord," will enter
the kingdom of heaven, but only the one who does the
will of my Father who is in heaven.

(Matthew 7:21)

The effectiveness of my (Greg's) service to God rests with admitting my sins and trusting that God will still want to use me. Confession removes barriers in my relationship to God that allows me to more fully love Him and be loved by Him. The second verse of the hymn "Amazing Grace" tells us why we must trust God:

T'was Grace that taught my heart to fear

And Grace, my fears relieved

How precious did that grace appear

The hour I first believed

Each of us is both saint and sinner, and the grace offered by Jesus' death can only be appreciated when we honestly admit our shortcomings and realize how far we have missed the mark for which we were created. Admitting our guilt is difficult. It takes courage to identify our debts and trespasses, and it is far easier to try to justify our sins to ourselves.

What is remarkable about God's grace is that He actively pursues us with His offer of salvation, using an eternal perspective that views us both in our current sinful state and also in our future glorified state. He sees us for what we are today and for what we will become. Understanding God's grace and trusting

Him involves knowing that He absolutely wants us to seek Him, and knowing that we absolutely don't deserve it.

If we see ourselves as being basically good, then grace doesn't have much meaning in our lives. If we see God as being "in the business of forgiving," then He isn't doing anything special by forgiving us. It is only in understanding our natural state that we can truly appreciate the difference. It can happen only when we understand that He is the perfect judge, that God's wrath is just as real as God's love, and that we "get it" and give God the thanks and the trust He deserves.

The first man who came to our ministry houses refers to himself as our "crash test dummy" because we didn't have a clue about how to go about helping men transition out of prison. He was the only guest we had for the first three months. God was taking it easy on us in the early part of our ministry by giving us just one person at a time.

Benjamin, the house manager at Covenant House, took him everywhere. He rode along in the van to the store or supermarket, to do odd jobs repairing things for people who had called Benjamin, and anywhere else Benjamin went. We weren't sure we should leave him at the house by himself—it always seemed that we should be doing more. There were probably times when he just wanted to be left alone, but that didn't curb our enthusiasm.

The man was sure we were up to something, but he just couldn't figure it out. I remember him watching me when we had our weekly meetings, and he later told me that he was always ready for the other shoe to drop. As he would say, "Nobody does this for nothing." It took him three months to realize I was serving God, not him, even though he thought he got all the benefit. We continue to be in touch with each other, and he frequently comes to our family events as an elder statesman of our ministry.

The man had been in prison for a violent crime, was released, and went right back to prison after reoffending. He had missed raising his family and wanted to reconcile with his wife. In the beginning, his wife wasn't too sure she wanted to be reconciled to him, because she saw that he hadn't changed much in that time he was between sentences. She did not know that he became active in the prison chapel during his last years in prison, and that it was from the chaplain that he got information about our program. She eventually noticed the difference and they reconciled, and they are happy being with each other and their family, including lots of grandchildren.

Trust is something that comes with time. It took a while for the man to trust me, and I think it's when he realized that my goal was to trust and serve God that he began to let his guard down. If my goal was only to serve him, he'd still be suspicious of when I would attempt to cash in on the things I did for him. Trusting God means that I don't have to keep score, don't have to worry about outcomes, and don't have to worry about what happens tomorrow. All that matters is that I'm "in the game" and playing hard. On my good days, I'm able to remember this.

I love how an ambassador's work never gets old. We are excited for each man who comes to us because we get to make new friends and face new challenges. We're constantly learning about what it means to be human, both in terms of its admirable qualities and those qualities that aren't so admirable. We often say to each other, "You can't make this stuff up!"

There was a man who had an aunt who was friends with my sister. My sister told the aunt about our ministry and how her nephew would benefit from living in a supportive environment when he left prison. I passed along an application to my sister, who gave it to the aunt who gave it to the man. The man sent in an application, but the problem was that it was pretty clear he wasn't at all on the right page in terms of his faith. His answer to the question "When did you come to saving faith?" was answered with "I haven't in about ten to fifteen years," and his answer to the question about life goals involved wanting to make sure he had good karma.

As the man's release date was coming up, his aunt asked him if he had been accepted into our program, and he said "yes." When I heard this from my sister, I didn't know what to say, because I couldn't remember sending him an acceptance letter. What I remembered was being uncertain about this man, but I figured that I was sloppy in my record keeping.

During our intake interview, the man was Mr. Know-it-all. He knew all about the bus system in Columbus, all about where he could go for reentry help, and where he could find himself a job. It was pretty clear he didn't want much of our advice, just a place to live. At the end of the interview I mentioned to him that I didn't recall sending him an acceptance letter. His response was, "You didn't—I just told my aunt that I was accepted so she'd stop bothering me."

The man didn't stay with us very long. He came in drunk a few times, and smoked in the house down in the basement behind the furnace so evidence of cigarette butts was harder to find. Smoking is a trigger for other behaviors that get men into trouble, which is why we don't want it in the houses. After he left, we would see him on Sunday mornings at the breakfast ministry for the homeless, and he called once in a while to see if I could give him a ride somewhere. Part of our ministry is being OK with not seeing a harvest in each person in our program but knowing that we showed each person God's love. We grow through each experience even if the men we serve don't seem to change. We grow when we remember our own shortcomings and trust that God will use us according to His plan.

His Amazing Grace

We're in and out, good, then bad . . .
    We're up and then we're down
What would life be like for us
    if God were not around?

God knew that we would need Him,
    for He knew what we would face
He knew that we could not survive
    without "Amazing Grace"

He knew that we had weaknesses
    through flesh and through sensation
Where each and every one of us
    have had our conversation (Ephesians 2:3)

We've lied, begrudged . . . been the judge,
    and quick to start a fuss
God knew that we would need Him
    in a world that's full of . . . "us"

His grace is with us everywhere,
    in everything we do
In ways we can't imagine . . .
    nor do we have a clue

We all would like to be the one
     who's known to get things done
But sometimes we can't be there . . .
     and just can't be the one

When we can't do our duties,
     He'll put someone in our place
To keep the fires burning
     and to keep us in the race

He knows that when we're full of pride,
     that pride will make us stumble
He also knows His loving grace
     will prove to make us humble

The grace of God is all we need
     to keep our lives on track
Once you understand this love,
     there is no turning back

All grace is a gift from God;
     there is no other kind
Acknowledge it . . . and keep it
     in the forefront of your mind

Amazing grace, how sweet the sound,
     that saved a wretch like me
I once was lost but now I'm found,
     was blind but now I see

Through many dangers, toils, and snares,
     we have already come
T'was grace that brought us safe thus far,
     and grace will lead us home

God knew that you'd be reading this,
no matter what your place
He wants you to consider Him,
and His amazing *grace*

Be Transformed by Faith in Christ

Whoever does God's will is my brother and sister
and mother.

(Mark 3:35)

Spiritual battles are always around us, but they are greatly intensified when a person first decides to follow Christ. Doubts enter our minds about our worthiness, whether God is actually calling us, and whether we can change and be used as instruments of His will. Our worst sins are immediately brought to our minds as we decide if God is really the author of our lives. We realize the depth of our sins, and at the same time realize the infinite holiness of God. How can we possibly respond to God's call?

We can't, without God's help. We submit ourselves to God when we stop resisting Him. As He draws us near to Him at the cross, He repairs our broken relationship and shows us the way back home. We take a sober assessment of ourselves and grieve the poverty of our spirit—our lack of ability to produce anything of spiritual worth. We let go of our pride, humble ourselves, and are then lifted up.

Submit yourselves, then, to God. Resist the devil,
and he will flee from you. Come near to God and he
will come near to you. Wash your hands, you sinners,

and purify your hearts, you double-minded. Grieve, mourn and wail. Change your laughter to mourning and your joy to gloom. Humble yourselves before the Lord, and he will lift you up. (James 4:7–10)

The process of sanctification starts as we give up our will and take on God's. As we are changed into His likeness, temptations arise and threaten our relationship with God. What are we to do?

The Bible talks about three types of temptation: the lust of the flesh, the lust of the eyes, and the pride of life (1 John 2:16). Lusts of the flesh may involve drug use, sexual sins, and even physical violence. Men coming out of prison have spent years in close quarters with other men spending a lot of time lifting weights, running around the track, and trying to stay fit. Many of the men who come to us are in great shape and want to show off their guns (i.e., big arms), and wear tight-fitting shirts and try to stand out. Others just want to run roughshod over others.

One of the men who came to our ministry was a total grouch. He was grumpy and snarling and absolutely the most disagreeable person I've ever met. He was mad about everything and couldn't understand why he didn't get what he wanted when he wanted it. When his roommate left his clock radio on, he unplugged it rather than turn down the volume to "teach him a lesson." When he left the door open as he left the house, he claimed he shut it even though everyone knew otherwise. When someone asked him if they could cook him eggs for breakfast, they weren't cooked right. Nothing was right, everything was wrong, and it was an outrage that everyone else didn't see it his way.

We finally couldn't put up with it anymore, and I had to have a talk with him. He told me that evil was present in the house and in the ministry, but that only he could see it. The implication was that we needed him more than we knew and that he was vital to our survival. I thought our conversation was like watching some grade B horror movie, and when I told him I was willing to take my chances without his advice, he just looked up toward heaven. I couldn't believe anyone would fall for something like that, especially since it was so poorly acted out. He eventually left in a huff to move to the YMCA downtown, but not until he cleaned out the cupboard of all of our cake mixes.

Lust of the eyes is coveting or anything that causes us to want something that isn't ours. We can covet after cars, houses, beautiful women, and just about anything that catches our attention. The lust of the eyes is about one's mind rather than about one's flesh.

Another man came into our ministry by reaching out directly to my church. The youth pastor knew him before he was incarcerated, and when he got out, he showed up to a church service and didn't have anywhere to stay. He had a rocky childhood, like many of the guys we get. He was young, thin, had a lot of tattoos, and was missing some of his teeth because of addiction. He also considered himself a good looker and a ladies' man, and didn't hesitate to remind us of this.

We do our best to tell the men that servanthood means that you abandon yourself. The moment we start thinking about how great we are, or how handsome we are, or how great a thing we're doing, we've lost our connection to God. I think that coveting can include our love for ourselves, because once we've given ourselves to God, we aren't ours anymore.

The pride of life rests with our desire to be famous and feel valuable. We sometimes get men into our ministry with dispro-portionately large egos. One man came with what he thought was a calling to do rap gospel music in Texas. He was single-minded about it, even when I tried to tell him that a person's calling is always to Christ, not to Texas. We may be sent to Texas, but we're called to Christ.

Another man liked to look good. It was important to him to have nice clothes and he would bring back suits to the house from thrift stores and church clothing rooms. He even was able to get a used tuxedo from a men's shop. He ran out of room to hang his suits in his bedroom, but found a wooden locker with a steel mesh front panel that we let him keep in the garage. There must have been ten suits in that locker. The problem was that the garage had a strong smell of gasoline from the lawnmower kept in there, and so the suits started to smell like gasoline, too. When he went to church, everyone knew he was coming.

Our transformation from our old self to an ambassador requires us to trust God so that we can do His will. We become brothers in Christ with others in service and rely on the Bible for instruction:

> For the word of God is alive and active. Sharper than any double-edged sword, it penetrates even to divid-ing soul and spirit, joints and marrow; it judges the thoughts and attitudes of the heart. (Hebrews 4:12)

One man who came to us had trouble sleeping through the night. He had scars on his wrists showing the number of times he had cut himself because of inner turmoil. He also spoke in full paragraphs as if he were giving a speech and he didn't listen well. He tried to pretend he was above all the hurt he felt and projected an aloof attitude.

Nonetheless, he knew he was in a safe place and slowly he opened up to God. At first, he helped out doing jobs around the house that were above and beyond the normal cleaning we have the men do. Then he developed relations with the other men in the house. He quit his job as an automobile detailer (i.e., cleaning cars) where he worked for an abusive boss, and found a much better job in maintenance at an apartment complex where he has worked for the last four years. He allowed God to change him.

Easter

Easter is a special time,
    that joyful time of year
When winter is behind us,
    and warmer days are here
A time that calls for Easter eggs,
    for almost everyone
We've boiled them and colored them . . .
    and had a lot of fun

It was "church" on Easter Sunday,
    as everybody knows
And some of us were blessed . . .
    to be dressed in brand new clothes
As kids we didn't understand
    what Easter is about
Most of us (as children)
    didn't feel like finding out

But now we are adults today . . .
    with children of our own
Some of them are little ones . . .
    and some completely grown
Let's take a look at Easter now,
    and contemplate the facts
Considering a loving God . . .
    examining our tracks

What does Easter mean to us?
    How do we now relate?
Do we understand the truth . . .
    or do we still debate?
Think about the timing
    that our God has put to use
A time for binding to the grave . . .
    a time for being loosed

A time for things to come to life . . .
    a time for things to die
A worm that dies in its cocoon
    comes out a butterfly
A seed that we may plant today
    will one day be a tree
Just like it is in nature . . .
    it's the same with you and me

By studying the Scripture
    we begin to understand
Why "death and resurrection,"
    are in the Master's plan

It wasn't just by accident
    that God would choose this season
For things to come to life again . . .
    He done this for a reason

What better time for Easter
    than to come in early Spring
When foliage begins to grow
    and birds begin to sing?
Trees and plants are growing leaves,
    and grass is turning green
New life is all around us . . .
    Do you know what I mean?

Just stop and take a look around,
    and see that things are changing
See the sky . . .the sun, the earth,
    that God is rearranging
Rains will come, revitalizing
    things that once were dead
To complete another cycle
    so that time can move ahead

We too have another cycle;
    we must die to self . . .
We have to take this flesh of ours . . .
    and put it on the shelf
Easter brings a message,
    that God wants us to know
If we really want a new life . . .
    we must let the old life *go*

Jesus let us know that we
    don't have to fear the grave
That's why we call Him "Savior" . . .
    that's why they call us "saved"
We're saved from all the fears
    of what will happen when we die
We have the chance to live again . . .
    and He's the reason why

We should be more than happy,
    with what our Lord has done
He rose up from the grave . . .
    giving *hope* to everyone
That's what Easter is all about,
    our *hope* in Jesus Christ
To give us hope and faith and trust . . .
    He was our sacrifice

There is nothing wrong with new outfits,
    or a brand-new Easter bonnet
There is nothing wrong with tables
    set with Easter baskets on it
Or with colored eggs and jellybeans
    and chocolate bunnies, too
But let us not forget about . . .
    what Christ has done for you

He came out from that grave alive,
    just like the Scriptures said
Resurrected! . . . Back to life! . . .
    To wake up what was dead

That faith in Him . . . that trust in Him . . .
     that *hope* we now can keep
He rose up from the dead
     for us to wake up from our sleep

Easter is a masterpiece
     of timing, love, and powers
God let us know that eternal life
     is absolutely ours
So let us welcome Easter
     as our faith in Jesus grows
Let us all remember what
     His resurrection shows

It shows we have the power
     to conquer life and death
So we can live in victory
     as long as we have breath
Let this day remind us
     of what our Lord has done
He has *"evidenced"* our future . . .
     giving *hope* to everyone

All of us should be convinced . . .
     there's nothing left to doubt
Giving thanks to Jesus
     is what Easter is about
And if you do not know Him . . .
     your life is incomplete
If you do, please offer Him . . .
     to everyone you meet.

Discussion Questions

1. Do you find your service to God tiring?

2. Do you fear God?

3. Do you see yourself as basically good, basically bad, or something else? Does your answer depend on whether you are thinking of yourself physically or spiritually?

4. Describe a time in your life where trust was broken. How long did it take to repair that trust? Is it fully repaired? If so, how was this accomplished?

5. Do you speak more than you listen? What don't people seem to be hearing?

6. How have you shown others that you trust God? What difficulties did you encounter?

7. Have you seen or experienced a delayed harvest in someone else? What happened for that person to come to his or her right mind?

8. How have you been tempted to help in the transformation of someone else in a way that was not, or would not have been, productive?

Chapter 5

DO NOT BE ANXIOUS

God is in control; He connects things in a way that we as human beings cannot tell. This is what I (Timothy) am learning as I watch what my lovely wife Happiness is doing for the children of Arusha, as well as through my own work with the children of Raranya.

I am witness to how God provides to His people. Here in Arusha, at Camp Moses and Camp Joshua, as well as at Leaders School in Raranya, we have children who come from impoverished families. How God touched us to minister to these children who come from these families is amazing.

My wife Happiness was touched in her heart as we were walking in Arusha. She saw a beggar cooking on the roadside, holding on her lap an uncovered little baby. Happiness went to that beggar and asked for that baby. She sat down, covered the baby with her *kanga*, and asked the beggar to leave her there; Happiness would cook and take care of everything, and let the woman go to beg.

When the beggar returned, she found everything was good. Happiness was ready to leave, but received a message from God to attend to the underprivileged and homeless children. That is how she started LOHADA (Loving Hand for Disadvantaged and Aged). LOHADA (Lohada.org) is doing very well in raising children who once had no direction, no destiny for their lives. Now these same children are doing very well; some are in primary schools, some in secondary schools, and some in colleges. Their performance is good both spiritually, mentally, and in terms of character.

God spoke to me as well when we started missions work at Raranya and showed me that to have a sustainable missions program for the Raranya people we needed to raise a new generation saturated in Christ. In 2015 we took a number of children from destitute families and started raising them. We have Leaders School, where the number of children now is 237, and we see Christ in each of them.

When God spoke to us about working with impoverished families, straight away we discovered the purpose and the meaning of our lives. We see it worthy to minister to needy people, needy children. We see ourselves planting a lifetime solution for people—that is, Jesus in a generation that will impact the world. We thank God who made this opportunity for us; serving these children and destitute families is the means for our daily satisfaction.

When our friend Godson came to Christ, the whole of his family stood against him; he was then excommunicated from his family. Godson did not give up. He went out and found a friend who could accommodate him. By then Godson was in Class VII at school, at twelve years of age. He continued loving and following Christ, and by God's immeasurable grace Godson was able to continue with school and obtain his CPA degree.

Currently, Godson is a senior church elder in one of the Tanzania Assemblies of God churches, one of the big bosses in the institution he is working with, and runs his own accountancy classes. His mother has come to Christ, and he is the one their family depends on now.

Normally, threats don't come from human beings, but threats do come from Satan. Human beings are just being used by Satan as his tools. It is good to understand, as Godson did, that people cannot harm those who accept Jesus to be their Savior and Master; however, behind the scenes, Satan wants to ensure that no one gets saved. We hear reports about people being threatened to turn from Jesus, but many have stood firm irrespective of all persecutions.

We saw the heart of Godson. Though he was mistreated, his heart did not change; instead, he continues to give unconditional love to his mother and relatives. Godson continues to embrace the love of God. The cruelty of his relatives did not change his heart, for his heart was filled with the love of Jesus Christ. Instead of taking revenge, he loves them. Instead of revenge, he assists them, and God has raised him for His glory. Godson has continued to stand with God's work wherever he is required to do so. He is a generous giver when it comes to missions work and helping the needy ones.

Ambassadors are not anxious about the necessities of daily life nor the threats of man, and they embrace mercy and forgiveness.

About Necessities of Daily Life

Therefore I tell you, do not worry about your life, what you
will eat or drink; or about your body, what you will wear.
Is not life more than food, and the body more than clothes?

(Matthew 6:25)

Numbers 13 reports on the Jewish nation's expedition into
Canaan to see what the land was like, to see if the towns were
fortified and whether they would encounter much resistance
when they would take what the Lord promised them. Twelve
men, one from each tribe, were sent on a reconnaissance mission. They came back with a report that the land was bountiful
but that the inhabitants were too strong to defeat. Only Joshua
and Caleb were ready to take them on. When the people heard
this report, they grumbled and complained:

> That night all the members of the community raised
> their voices and wept aloud. All the Israelites grum-
> bled against Moses and Aaron, and the whole assem-
> bly said to them, "If only we had died in Egypt! Or
> in this wilderness! Why is the LORD bringing us to
> this land only to let us fall by the sword? Our wives
> and children will be taken as plunder. Wouldn't it be
> better for us to go back to Egypt?" And they said to
> each other, "We should choose a leader and go back
> to Egypt." (Numbers 14:1–4)

God had brought his people out of bondage, protected them
as they crossed the Red Sea, gave them a pillar of fire at night
and a pillar of cloud during the day, water to drink, and food

to eat. He spoke to the people of Israel, and promised them a future inheritance. Then, just when the going looked like it was getting tough, they started to bicker and complain.

This all seems pretty ridiculous as we look back at it. But it is a reminder of how each of us bickers and complains as God works in our lives despite the great work He does.

About ten years ago I (Greg) met a man who called the class administrator of the Monday night Bible study and said he wanted to attend. The problem was that he had just been released from prison, was staying at the Faith Mission, and was about to be homeless. He had no way of getting to the study.

The class administrator put the word out for someone to bring him to class and I volunteered. What ensued was a friendship that taught me many things: God can change the heart of any man; men coming out of prison often face exceptionally hard circumstances as they reestablish their lives; and, many of them have nowhere to go.

The man used to bring a carry-on suitcase with him when we went to Bible study that contained all of his possessions. One Monday during Bible study he wheeled his suitcase behind him as he went off to his small group discussion, and one of the other men in his group (not knowing he was homeless) asked him in a joking way what was in the suitcase. His response was, "everything." The man who asked the question was devastated, and went out to buy a sleeping bag for my homeless friend that night.

During the winter my friend didn't have any place to stay, so I contacted a storage facility downtown and rented a four-by-eight-foot storage locker. He spent the rest of the winter camping out in his locker to avoid the freezing weather. My friend suffered from diabetes and often found it hard to think clearly.

He also had difficulty finding employment because of his prison record.

As my wife and I got to know him, we became less afraid of being around people coming out of prison. He was our example that God could change anyone, and that God would direct and protect us as He did in so many stories in the Bible. Our friend helped us realize that men coming out of prison needed a place where they could reestablish their lives in a positive and secure environment, and he was instrumental in the establishment of our transition ministry.

My friend passed away a few years ago. I got a call from his sister and we went to his funeral. He moved back home when he started to encounter health issues because of his diabetes and wanted to be around family. His death was not expected, and in thinking back over our interactions during the five years that I knew him, I realize how little he bickered or complained. He had a deep faith in God and a peaceful spirit. He knew that God had brought him through much in his life and wasn't about to abandon him. His patience helps me to remember my blessings from God.

Are You Guilty?

Why do we complain so much,
    when things don't go our way?
Why is there so much negative
    in what we have to say?

We complain in our opinions
    about what is right or wrong
Joining conversations
    where we really don't belong

Arguing and bickering . . .
    unmindful of the cost
Damaging relationships
    to get our point across

Quick to murmur . . . quick to bicker . . .
    quick at finding blame
Quick expressing how we feel . . .
    quick to make our claim

Quickly finding something wrong,
    seven days a week
When we should be quick to listen . . .
    instead of quick to speak

Complaining of conditions
    that we cannot rearrange
We bicker, fuss, and argue
    over things we cannot change

We complain about the folks
    who may sin differently than us
It seems that all we do at times
    is finger-point and fuss

We bicker, grumble, and murmur
    using zero self-restraints
Stressed and overburdened
    with the clutter of complaints

Does some of this remind you
    of the person in the mirror?
If so, there is a book to read
    that makes things really clear!

Contentious, the Bible calls it . . .
      fussing without cease
Preferring *not* to get along . . .
      seldom seeking peace (Hebrews 12:14)

To live with a contentious person . . .
      is *never* one's desire
For they *will* spark up an argument . . .
      then put wood on the fire (Proverbs 26:21)

So let's be less contentious;
      let's not murmur and complain
Let's not challenge God with bickering . . .
      with nothing good to gain

God doesn't like complainers
      and we shouldn't find it odd
Murmuring against God's people . . .
      is murmuring against God

Do all things without murmuring
      and disputing . . . "shine your light"
And surely you can trust God
      to make things turn out right

About the Threats of Man

On my account you will be brought before governors and kings as witnesses to them and to the Gentiles. But when they arrest you, do not worry about what to say or how to say it. At that time you will be given what to say.

(Matthew 10:18–19)

I had the pleasure of teaching first and second graders in Bible study a few years ago. They were innocent, wanting to help, eager to respond, with their hands raised at every homework question. They would yell "Hi, Mr. Allenby!" in the hallway, and wanted to tell everyone how their week had been. We studied the books of Moses that year, and when we came to the story of Balaam's donkey in Numbers 22 the boys all wanted to act out being the donkey and the girls wanted to be the angel of the Lord.

In previous years I had taught middle schoolers, whose egos had emerged and some of their innocence had been lost. They didn't think it was very cool to raise their hands, and getting them to share their answers was a little more challenging. They were anxious about being different from the others.

Our egos emerge in late elementary school years as we assert our individuality and wonder how we fit into this world; we become competitive. I remember my son talking about not being one of the cool kids in his middle school. He listed about six groups of kids (tough kids, athletes, band members, theater kids, etc.) and spoke about the pecking order at school. It broke my heart that my son, whom God created, would in some way think he was worth less than the other kids. Along any one dimension, we can be ranked—some of us are faster or stronger, or better at math or music—but it's impossible to be the best at everything or the worst at everything.

I was an adult leader of a confirmation class at my church for a number of years. The class was for seventh-grade students who were there to confirm their faith. One child in the class was very disruptive the entire year. He would speak out in class, not do his homework, and generally was a pain in the neck. At the end of the year, when the class was to stand before the congregation and confess their faith, this child blurted out that he wasn't going to confess anything.

I took him into the church sanctuary and asked him what was wrong. He told me that he was sure that God didn't love him. When I asked why he thought this, he said, "Because He made me stupid." This young man was dealing with a lot of things, including being held back in school and the divorce of his parents, besides the usual trauma of middle school. I told him that he was precious in God's eyes, and that none of us knows what God has in store for us when we're older. I told him that the hard times of our lives are used for our good by God (Romans 8:28), and that the things he was currently experiencing made him better equipped to be a soldier in God's army. I believe the words I expressed were from God (I couldn't have thought this up so quickly), and that he found comfort in them in knowing that there was a purpose for his life and a higher reason for his suffering.

It takes many of us a lifetime to realize that God's ways are higher than our ways, and that we simply need to trust and have faith. A big change in my faith journey came when I realized that God is the God of all things, not just the God of good things.

> When times are good, be happy; but when times are bad, consider this: God has made the one as well as the other. (Ecclesiastes 7:14a)

God knows we will fail, we will sin, we will fall short, and yet He still tells us to come to Him as children. As adults, we are a mess of insecurities and worries. We want to be respected and prove our worth. We often try to control things we shouldn't, and desperately want to figure things out. But spiritual things cannot be reasoned through before the fact, only after the fact (Matthew 11:25), and when we try to be wise and adultlike we don't get anywhere.

When God looks at us, He simultaneously sees us in our present condition and in our future glory. He knows exactly who we are and what we will become, and He loves us for being both. He calls out to us and asks us to trust Him. We need to come to Him as enthusiastic children, not adults who want to be in charge. God doesn't make any mistakes as He establishes His ambassadors.

One Man's Testimony

The following story comes from one of the men who came to our ministry looking for help. His story is similar to many of the stories men have in our ministry, and illustrates the uphill battle they face in life and as they come out of prison. He continues to stay in touch with us and is doing well.

$$*\qquad*\qquad*$$

I have been through much as a child; I was isolated, physically, verbally, and emotionally abused. I was raised by mother and stepfather. Love was not shown and communication did not exist. I was on the street at the age of fifteen. I did not know who I was or were I belonged. I started associating with anyone who would pay attention to me; it was always the wrong people. I started drinking, dropped out of school, and eventually gained the attention of the legal system. I ended up at the age of eighteen locked up in a jail psych ward. It took seven years of therapy and seven years of court supervision to get me to function in society. Just going to an AA meeting would throw me into panic attacks.

I was an emotional wreck. Once I was stabilized, I began to work and became self-sufficient and productive, until I started a relationship. My girlfriend was like the old me; she was also like my stepdad. We were together for fifteen years and she was equally abusive, especially when drinking. Once again, I spiraled down. We have one child together and I raised him best I could, but he witnessed a lot of fighting between his mother and me.

She introduced me to drugs in 2005 and I reluctantly accepted; wow, what a wonderful way to escape all the hurt. After five years I found out what hurt was all about. The drugs took over my life. It was first above anything, including my family. At the end I was disgusted, depressed, hopeless, scared, angry, helpless, and homeless. The only way out for me was suicide.

Now clinically speaking, I should be dead; I was in the intensive care unit for a week and the doctors said I might not wake up. If I did wake up, they said, I wouldn't be able to speak, and I would have brain damage.

It was then and there that I knew God existed. I woke up. I was able to talk. I was able to walk. I was alive! There was no other way to explain why I lived. I joined a Christian program and started going to church. The message that day spoke directly to me; I felt this warming sensation flowing through me from head to toe and I cried liked never before. The pastor asked if anyone wanted to come forward and receive Christ; I did. Then they asked me if I would like to be baptized; I did. I did not think they meant for me to be baptized right away, but before I knew it, I was declaring my life to Jesus in front of a congregation of at least five hundred.

Many great things started to happen from that point. I met great Christian friends and started to develop a relationship with God; however, I was not finished dealing with my sin. God knew this too, of course. I started using again, violated my probation, and went to prison for ten months. It was there that I completely surrendered to God.

On my knees in that cold cell, locked down twenty-three hours a day, I cried out to God: "Take it all, Lord; here is my heart, here is my life. I cannot do this anymore. Teach me, mold me, and make me a new person. I only want your will for me, let it be done." I started to attend a ministry called Reformers Unanimous. It is a faith-based addiction program. It was through this ministry that God really started to move in my life. I learned about the state of complete surrender to Jesus Christ as Lord and Savior of my life. I began for the first time to really get into the Word of God. I could not stop reading my Bible. I prayed for a strong desire for His Word, and my thirst became insatiable. The words were alive. Something was happening and I felt so much different. My chains were breaking.

When I went to prison, I was estranged from my family. I had no way to contact anyone, and no one knew where I was. I started thinking about my son, my dad, and my brother. I remembered feeling so empty and alone. I prayed to God that He would help me open the lines of communication with my family. A week later I received a letter from my brother, then a letter from my dad. The best was a letter from my son, wishing me a happy Father's Day. My dad had been praying for me many years. He was so excited to hear that I turned my life over to Jesus. I continued to attend various church functions while in prison. Each and every time, God spoke to me. I developed a more intimate relationship with Him. I was growing and learning so much about Jesus, my personal Lord and Savior. I thank God that He allowed me to spend the time in prison. He knew what it would take; I had my back in every corner and there was nowhere else to turn.

Upon release I had nowhere to go and no one to pick me up. I trusted in the Lord that He would, according to His promises, provide and make provisions for me. I thanked Him and prayed about that daily. He was quiet about this area of my life. It was not until I was a week away from being released when the Lord presented an open door. I never doubted Him. I knew in His timing He would guide me and protect me. I now realize that God was silent, and stood back, just to see how I would respond. Would I panic and do my will in this situation? No, I would not. God knows what is best for me, even during the times when things don't make sense; there is a big picture I cannot see. I was introduced to a Christian halfway house and they accepted me. The people that I have been blessed with have so much love for the Lord and others.

God sure knows what is best for me. Since I have been out, I reconnected with the Reformers Unanimous Program. It is held at church that also has become my home church, this church I love so much. The pastor, members, and the entire congregation are genuine Christians with reverence for the Lord. This church also stands on the Word of God and truly is concerned about bringing others to Jesus.

Now, I believe in the power of intercession. Everything that I give to the Lord He has given back even better. I prayed while I was away that the Lord would take care of my son since I could not be there for him. Most importantly, I prayed that the Lord would place someone in his life that would help him turn to Jesus. I talked to him when I got out and he said: "Dad, I believe in Jesus; I go to church, and I have been baptized." Praise God! I must have cried for a half hour when I hung up with my boy.

God gave me back my son, even better. I gave the Lord my heart of stone, full of regret, anger, loneliness, and a wall built around it completely closed off to others. He gave me back a heart that reaches out to others with love; it's a heart that is so in love and on fire for God. He gave me my heart back. It is a brand-new heart that is soft, compassionate, joyful, peaceful, and I have started to develop love for everyone.

I now wake up thanking God for my life. I wake up excited to serve God and I'm always happy to be awake and so energized and ready to accomplish. I used to always be worried about things, how will I do this or that, where will I find a place to live, how am I going to feed myself and my family, why do I always do the wrong thing; things were so bad I would wake up actually regretting it. Now I have an inner peace that surpasses all understanding; I know that God is on my side and that if I wait for Him, He will open doors no one can close.

As well, it used to take me an hour to fall asleep and my nights were so fitful. Now I lay down and I'm asleep in minutes and I sleep all night without waking. I happily wake up early and spent two hours with the Lord every morning without the use of an alarm clock. The Lord truly is the Lord of restoration.

I stay surrendered to him in all things and I am not anxious for anything. I now am rooted and stand firmly on the Word of God. Now, I am not saying I'm perfect and my life is always going to be easy. I understand that I will still go through storms, but it will be different because I will hold on to God even harder, knowing that there is a reason and that it will all work out for His glory. It's such a comfort to know that God loves His children so much that He gave His only Son to die for us. He will not leave us, and He will not forsake us.

The choice is ours. God will not force Himself upon us. As for me, I choose life. I choose truth. I choose to serve God and others by spreading the love the Lord has for me. I will not cover my light; I will let it shine for the world to see. Thank God for my new life. My strength comes only from God who created the heavens and the earth. It has only begun, and I cannot wait to see what the Lord has in store for the future.

Embrace Mercy and Forgiveness

> *Then Peter came to Jesus and asked, "Lord, how many times shall I forgive my brother or sister who sins against me? Up to seven times?"*
>
> *Jesus answered, "I tell you, not seven times, but seventy-seven times."*

(Matthew 18:21–22)

There are two kinds of people in this world—those who believe that Christ is Lord, and those who do not. Jesus' ministry can be thought of as bringing people to this critical decision and then making them choose. The crowds loved Jesus when He fed them (John 6:15)—they were ready to make Him their king! But they left Him when they realized their possessions and relationships might need to be forsaken if He was truly to be their King (Matthew 8:20). Jesus didn't want to be their king; He wanted to be their King. There's a big difference.

The Bible is filled with contrasts such as this. We either walk in the light or we walk in the dark (1 John 1:6–7). We are either on the narrow path or we are on the wide path (Matthew 7:13–14). We will either line up on the right with the sheep, or on the left with the goats (Matthew 25:33). There is no third alternative. We either spend eternity in the presence of God, or we spend eternity in the absence of God. We are either increasing in wisdom and faith, or we are decreasing in wisdom and faith—no one just stays the same. If we do nothing, we backslide. It's that simple. It is an uphill battle for us to remain in God, and we've got to work at it.

At some point in our lives, each of us comes to the conscious decision of what type of person we want to be. And, as you might expect, there are just two choices. The first choice involves a life of service. We decide that we want to serve others, and not just physically. We learn that giving is gaining, and we learn that the situations put before us are opportunities to do God's work. We may not know how all the pieces of the story fit together, but we know with certainty that God does have a plan and that we want to be part of it. We look to God for guidance, and trust that there is a bigger purpose to the little things we do in life. We know with certainty that in the end, God wins. We are willing to deny ourselves and to take up our crosses (Mark 8:34), in service for God's kingdom as His ambassadors.

The second choice involves a life of consumption. For these people, the world is an oyster for their taking. Life is good when they feel good, and money is thought to bring happiness. They do their own thing. When confronted with their own bad behavior, their usual reply is that no one told them they couldn't or shouldn't do it. They believe that God doesn't care about the little things we do wrong—He wants us to have fun and be popular.

There is a big difference between these two choices. The first one involves reaching out in service to others, and the second involves using others for our own advancement. They cannot coexist—each of us eventually needs to choose one way of living or the other. Saint Francis of Assisi chose the first and prayed: "Lord, make me an instrument of your peace."

Every Tuesday evening at our in-house Bible study at Fort Jackson, we begin the night with dinner and fellowship. I (Greg) stop at the grocery store on my way from work, pick up the food and begin preparing the meal at about 5 p.m. There's salad to prepare and chicken to marinate, and the men bring the grill out of the garage onto a concrete slab that we call the "plateau of reason." In good weather, men gather around the grill and we talk about life. It's one of the best times of my week.

One evening last summer we were having our grill-side chat on the plateau of reason, when the parole board decided to do a surprise inspection. A car rolled up and two parole officers got out. I was glad to see them; we work hard at keeping the parole board up to date on house activities. I gave them a wave and invited them into our circle.

I didn't expect to see the change in countenance in the men around the grill. Their faces turned solemn and their conversation stopped. Even though the officers were friendly—and, in my opinion, nonthreatening—their presence had a profound effect on the group. The men absolutely did not want these people anywhere near them. They didn't respond to a simple "hello" from the officers, and when one of the officers asked a person's name who was an alumnus of our ministry, he responded by saying, "I'm not part of the program."

I've never seen such a universal change in demeanor of a group of people. Prison is a traumatic experience that doesn't disappear when men are released. The animosity between inmate and officer continues outside the prison grounds and may take years to overcome. While we all need to see our enemies as imperfect human beings who can be made perfect by Christ, officers still have authority over the lives of parolees and are a perceived threat to their well-being. Embracing mercy and forgiveness is sometimes difficult.

Lord, Show Me the Way

Do I give more than take, and is that a mistake . . .
    do I burden or lighten one's load?

Can I live like I've been, like most other men . . .
    who travel the more traveled road?

I do want to share, in your love and your care . . .
    not my flesh and my spirit collide

Now your wonderful voice, is giving me choice . . .
    and I know it is time to decide

I confess that I know which way I should go . . .
    and I am getting stronger each day

As I open my heart, to engage a new start . . .
    Lord, come in and show me the way.

Discussion Questions

1. If you had to pack your belongings into a carry-on suitcase, what would you make sure to include?

2. What do you complain about most?

3. Do you know someone who doesn't bicker and complain? Why do you think they don't do this?

4. What do people in your community complain about most? Why?

5. How do you serve those who live a life of consumption without feeling that you are being abused?

6. What traumatic experience have you had in your life that affects your ability to be used by God? How can this negative effect be turned into a positive effect?

7. Why do people doubt the love and provision of God? How can you be helpful in this regard?

8. What is the hardest part of embracing mercy and forgiveness?

Chapter 6

BE HOLY

We need to know that we were created in the image and likeness of God (Genesis 1:26–27) and that we have an origin of holiness. Sin corrupted and marred our holiness but did not remove it, and salvation is the starting point of going back to our origin of holiness. A person needs to allow Jesus Christ to come in him to wash and clean the heart by His blood that He shed on the cross. It's like scrubbing rusted metal with steel wool until the metal becomes clean, without any stain.

Accepting Christ as your Savior and Master is the starting point. Thereafter we are asked to develop a passion for reading and studying the Bible, a passion for personal prayer, a passion for fellowship with fellow born-again Christians and to attend church services—all of which helps us to reach our origin of holiness as we enjoy intimacy with God.

In Tanzania, like other countries, we (Timothy) are blessed with different kinds of fruits. One can learn how people cherish trees that bear good fruit. When it is a season for mango trees to bear fruit, people will be on those trees all the time, reaping mangoes. If it is a season for the avocado trees to bear fruits, the avocado trees will all have people surrounding them looking for avocados.

Farmers always give tender care to the plants that bear good fruit. They make sure the plant gets enough water, good soil, good protection from any corruption, any diseases. They will always be close to that plant because they want, at the end of the day, to get good fruit out of it.

The same applies to our relationship with God. He knows what He has deposited in us. We have good fruits in us, only sin has corrupted our internal system. Instead of bearing good fruit, the corrupted system made us bear bad fruit.

Now that you have accepted Jesus Christ as your personal Savior, your corrupted system has been replaced by a new holy system, by God's divine grace you are expected to bear good fruits. You will just find yourself having a passion for prayer, reading and studying the Bible, visiting those in prison and in hospitals, helping the needy, and much more. You will find yourself sense the freshness of the Holy Spirit in your life in amazing ways. Pray that this becomes real in your life.

> Ambassadors have clean hearts and
> bear good fruit.

Clean the Inside of the Cup

> *Jesus said to them, "Be on your guard against the yeast*
> *of the Pharisees and Sadducees."*
>
> (Matthew 16:6)

A hymn that I (Greg) like is "For the Beauty of the Earth." It praises God for the beauty of His creation and His plan of salvation. The sixth verse of this song gives thanks for Jesus: "For thyself, best Gift Divine, to the world so freely given. . . ."

God's gift of His Son Jesus is often expressed this way—as a free gift to us. We have all heard this expression and are reminded of it almost every time we attend a church service. Jesus died on the cross and bore our sin so that we could be in right standing with God. All that we need to do is to accept this gift, and we are forgiven and are granted eternal life. Yet, if it is really that simple, why do so many of us continue to struggle with our sin?

I think there are two reasons: 1) we underestimate the cost of this gift to God; and 2) we underestimate the cost to ourselves of claiming it. While the gift of Jesus is offered freely, there is still an enormous cost of accepting Him into the depths of our being. The gift of Christ, or grace, is not like the presents we find on Christmas morning. It is infinitely valuable and infinitely costly. It is literally the best and most difficult present we can claim.

Let's first think about the cost to God. God is holy and without sin. Sin cannot survive the presence of God, just as darkness cannot survive the presence of light. Moses asked to see God and was told that no one can see His face and survive (Exodus 33:20–23). Moses was placed in a cleft of rock on Mount Sinai and only a portion of God passed in front of him—and that was enough to significantly alter Moses' physical appearance (Exodus 34:29). When the Israelites were wandering in the desert, doing things that were detestable to Him, God warned Moses that further misdeeds would result in His departure for fear of destroying the young Israelite nation (Exodus 33:3). The very nature of God—holy and just—means that sin can only be dealt with in one way in His presence: total obliteration.

Now consider the concept of Jesus taking on the sins of the world, and couple this thought with the thought that Jesus and God are the same. Throughout the Gospel of John, Jesus claims to be God. Not with God, like God, or a person that knows God, but God Himself.

This is expressed in John 1:1: "In the beginning was the Word, and the Word was with God, and the Word was God."

When the Pharisees questioned Jesus about who He was in John 8:58: "'Very truly I tell you,' Jesus answered, 'before Abraham was born, I am.'"

And again at the death of Lazarus in John 11:25–26: "I am the resurrection and the life. The one who believes in me will live, even though they die; and whoever lives by believing in me will never die."

Jesus is not claiming to know the secret to eternal life. He is claiming that He *is* the life.

So how can God, who is holy and just, take on the sin of the world without obliterating Himself? Jesus did not want to be forsaken (Matthew 27:46) and abandoned because of sin, but endured this horrible pain for us two thousand years ago as an expression of His love for us today. Grace is freely given to us, but it was not freely obtained. God seriously wants us to come back to Him and has paid the highest price for our freedom—much higher than the debt we owe for any offense we have committed.

I'm reminded of a story of a father who had two children. God tells the father that he must choose which of his children goes to heaven and which goes to hell. The father tells God that this decision is too difficult for him. God persists and tells the father to choose. The father tells God that he is incapable of making such a choice, but God continues to ask him to choose. God finally insists that the father make the choice and the father says that he cannot. The father then says that, because of his love for his children, that he would rather die in their place and says,

"Take me instead." I like to think that I would do this for my children, and I know this is what Christ has done for me.

A second reason we falter in receiving grace is that we fail to be explicit about the sins for which we seek forgiveness. There is a misconception that the burden of our sins is done away with once we claim Christ, without needing to be explicit about which misdeeds and bad thoughts need to be purged from our record. Our sins must be explicitly lifted up to God if we are to be free from them. Admitting our sins happens when we let God into our "secret" place of denial where we've justified our actions. Once we allow God to enter, He will heal us, but if He is not admitted we will continue to be stuck in our guilt.

Some of our sins might involve rebellion against God because of the situation we're currently in. If so, then we should consider ourselves fortunate to know what it is that we've done wrong. A person is much worse off if they cannot or will not identify their sins. Sins of omission (e.g., being in denial of one's bad behavior) comprise a dangerous state of being because it halts the process of receiving grace. Accepting forgiveness isn't easy—it hurts to know how sinful we truly are and recognize how frequently we do it.

A while back I was leading a men's group for homeless guys that took place right after a church service. We would serve some lunch and then go around the table and fellowship by talking about our week and how the sermon we all just heard spoke to us. One Sunday the sermon was related to sin, and I asked the question "How often do you sin?" I estimate that there are days when my frequency of sinning is so high that the number of sins I commit is in the hundreds. As we went around the room, one of the men had a funny expression on his face and said that he thought he sinned once, maybe twice a month. I couldn't believe what I was hearing. I asked him to clarify what he meant by this, and he stuck to his original answer. He didn't come to our men's group after that.

Being in relationship with God requires us to balance two thoughts that are absolutely true. The first thought is that God's love for us is infinite. His Son died for us so that we could be in relationship with Him without being destroyed. We need to know in our hearts, without a shadow of doubt, that His love is more than enough to deal with our desire to be independent of Him and our sins, however horrible we know them to be. He wants us to come back to Him. The second thought is that we are all sinners. This isn't an excuse—it's just the truth. I'm a sinner and so are you, and the sooner we both recognize our inherent desire to "do our own thing," the sooner we can ask for forgiveness so that we can come back to Him.

Grace is freely offered, but it was not freely obtained nor is it freely received. It costs a lot to be a Christian and give up your right to your life. It's painful to think specifically about the harm we've done to others and how we've turned our backs on God. But it's actually more harmful for us to pretend we never think about it—or worse yet, deny those thoughts from entering our consciousness. Freedom has its price, but the price of denial is much higher.

The ideal candidates for our ministry are men in their fifties and sixties who have been "around the mountain" enough times to know two things: 1) they need to change; and 2) time is running out. Everyone who comes to us starts out with great intentions, but their true nature isn't revealed to us until they have choices. This happens when they get a job and a car and money, and have freedom to either stay away from their old life or go back to it. It's very difficult to predict this ahead of time. Men can appear to be on the right track by studying their Bible and being an encouragement to others in the houses. But our experience is that they are really not tested until they deny themselves.

An alcoholic is compelled to stop drinking while they are in prison, but this doesn't mean that they've stopping being an alcoholic—it only means that they haven't had a drink for a while. They are just a "dry drunk" unless they truly clean the inside of their cup and stop imagining the pleasure of having a drink. This mindset is a private thing, and many men go back to their old ways because, in their hearts, they enjoy it and want to continue.

An early indication of being on the wrong path is a lack of progress on the right path. Every Saturday at our house meetings we have the men memorize a verse from the Bible and tell the rest of us how God has spoken to them that week. In the beginning the Bible verse and their experience are tightly connected. As time goes on, for some men, the connection is not so tight, and some men actually start repeating the same verse or saying the same thing every week. One man began saying that he enjoyed growing in "wisdom and knowledge" of God. This eventually became somewhat of a signature expression for him, but he did not stay with us very long after he started repeating it every week.

Another man found success in painting and even started his own painting business. He would come to the house meeting absolutely convinced that God had anointed him and raised him up to receive the blessing of a lucrative job. As the cash came in, his "praise" of God intensified and his conviction that he was blessed became unshakeable. It got to the point where he would say the same thing every week, raising himself up and implicitly putting down those who weren't blessed with jobs and money. In reality, he couldn't handle the money and he eventually found his way back to using crack cocaine. He wasn't willing to admit his struggle, and as a result we were not able to walk with him.

The Price of Freedom

What is the price of freedom?
    . . . If asked, what would you say?
To have this thing called "freedom,"
    what would you be willing to pay?
Well, freedom is a gift to us,
    which to many . . . makes no sense
To us it is freely given,
    but the cost to God was immense

For God can never look on sin . . .
    His pureness won't allow it
It is in His natural holiness
    to completely disavow it
And only through the sacrifice
    of His only begotten Son
Does He overlook the sins of ours . . .
    every . . . single . . . one

What an enormous price to pay
    for mankind to be free
God turned His back on Himself
    to give us freedom . . . you and me
He paid the highest price for us . . .
    He saves us through His grace
And in our ignorance, still,
    we sometimes slap Him in His face

Knowing that we do things
    that God does not approve
Like staying in a sinful space
    when God tells us to move
Or choosing to ignore His voice
    identifying our sin
Denying the reality
    of the fault that we are in

Choosing not to sacrifice
    the things that please the "self"
Or lifting up our righteousness,
    just to put it on the shelf
We must give up our "self"
    and come away from being lost
Grace is freely given
    (but indeed there is a cost)

Giving up the self
    is something most don't want to do
For we sin all the time,
    though you may doubt it . . . it is true
Many won't confess to this,
    but in our hearts . . . we know
That's why we get anxious
    when it comes our time to go

We know deep down inside
    we haven't done all that we could
Sometimes we are "A-okay" . . .
    then sometimes "not so good"
But friends we need to know
    what grace and mercy is about
God loves us in our sins
    beyond a shadow of a doubt

He's already paid
    for every sin that we commit
He paid the cost and faced
    the cross for our benefit
That's how much He loves us,
    and wants us by His side
He placed in us an area
    for His spirit to reside

Still we have a choice, we can
    accept this gift . . . or not
We can grab a hold to freedom . . .
    or choose bondage 'til we rot
The time will come to meet Him,
    and face judgment on that day
To enter into His freedom, then,
    how much would you pay?

Bear Good Fruit

*A good tree cannot bear bad fruit, and a bad tree
cannot bear good fruit.*

(Matthew 7:18)

There is only one requirement for being saved. It's not being perfect or sinless. There are no crimes against humanity that make it impossible for us to reach the kingdom of heaven. We only need to accept our salvation by grace through faith in Jesus Christ (Ephesians 2:8). That's the good news. The bad news is that not very many people place their faith in Christ. Instead, they try to manage their relationship with the Creator of the universe, not knowing how absurd that sounds.

Some people feel the need to get back to church or chapel after a period of absence to reconnect with old friends and get their spirits lifted. They might open the Bible after a spell of not reading it because it helps them center their lives. They might even do good deeds for others, because it helps them to stop feeling sorry for themselves. These things aren't necessarily bad, but they don't sound much like worship. They are too me-centered, and not God-centered.

God knows that the only true happiness we will ever have in this world comes from Him. He wants us to honor Him and be obedient to His commands. The only requirement for being saved is:

> If you declare with your mouth, "Jesus is Lord," and believe in your heart that God raised him from the dead, you will be saved. (Romans 10:9)

Declaring one's love for Jesus is easy. Making Him Lord of your life is difficult. It certainly doesn't involve management skills or the ability to negotiate one's relationship with the Creator. It means that we listen and obey. God wants us to put Him first in our lives and not second or third, or only sometimes first. We are told:

> The fear of the LORD is the beginning of wisdom, and knowledge of the Holy One is understanding. (Proverbs 9:10)

One of the things God told the Israelites is to honor Him with their firstfruits. A firstfruit is the first part of the harvest that produces the finest wine and grain. God wanted the Israelites to honor Him above themselves. They were also to honor the priest and Levites with firstfruits (Deuteronomy 18:4); and when the Israelites came back from exile, Nehemiah exhorted the people to rebuild the wall and to remember to return to Him the firstfruits of their labors (Nehemiah 10:35).

Our firstfruits are related to the natural gifts that God has given to us. Some of us are good at making money, and we should give lots of it to God. Some of us can make music or sing, and we should be singing for God. Others can write, listen, or organize, and we should be doing that for God. God has endowed us with natural talents, and we are called to use them for His glory.

Why do you think that God made some people poor and others rich? Some musically inclined and others tone deaf? Why did He make some people patient and some people high-energy? It's so that the people who "have" can give and minister to the people who "have not." He wants us to help each other, and since no one is the worst at everything, we always have someone to whom we can minister. And, since none of us are the best at everything, there is always someone who can minister to us.

The last thing that God wants is for us take our gifts and use them to stand apart from others. He doesn't want the person who is good at math to hoard that ability and not help others get through their math problems. He doesn't want the star football player to use his star status to remind others they don't have the same ability, nor to use this status in any way other than to honor God.

I know many people who get mad at the beggars on the freeway off-ramps who ask for money. Some of the beggars have signs saying, "God bless you," and it's not clear that they themselves love God. But we know that "The poor you will always have with you" (Matthew 26:11), and this is a reminder to us that God's gifts are not equally distributed in this world. I wish I could sing better, but I can't, and I need someone to help me carrying a tune. I love it when a person who can really sing stands next to me or behind me during a hymn so that I can do a better job. I imagine that this good singer isn't too thrilled to have a tone-deaf neighbor, but I appreciate his willingness to help me sing.

Ambassadors look for opportunities to share their gifts. This might look like an envelope containing a Bible and a granola bar that we give to the beggar on the freeway ramp, or it might be a tutoring session at a local school, or even money we put in our wallet for giving away during the day. God wants us to be holy, but also wants us to share. Mission reinforces our holiness, and our holiness reinforces our mission. You can't do one without the other.

Fruitfulness

What does it take to produce a good crop?
What does it take to bear fruit?
Well, we must take some time in preparing the field
So the seed will have chance to take root

Digging and turning and tilling your ground
. . . and getting it ready for seed
Having your soil both nurtured and moist
Making it fertile indeed

Sowing your seed when the timing is right
Watching and waiting for signs
Choosing with caution the seeds that you plant
(Fruit comes in all different kinds)

You know there are fruits of unrighteousness . . .
That we all have been tempted to plant
We all have at times done spiritual crimes
Though we wish to deny it . . . we can't

So we must seek the Spirit of Christ to discern
What type of fruit we will grow
There are all types of plants that will grow in this world
But remember . . . you'll reap what you sow

If you should sow the flesh, my friends
You will from that flesh, reap corruption
But if you should sow to the Spirit . . .
You'll reap life that's without interruption (eternal)

God has commissioned us all to bear fruit
Providing us each with the "seed"
Clearly and plainly our Bible's the source
Which we must take some time out to read

Spreading . . . teaching . . . planting . . . sowing . . .
And reaping the harvested crop
Praising the Lord for the fruit of our labor
Praying it never to stop

We know that it's God who gives us the seed
By planting *His Word* in our heart
If you wish to bear fruit and produce a good crop
His Word is the best place to start

Discussion Questions

1. What might be one of your sins of omission? Do you think others would agree with you?

2. How do you simultaneously balance the truth of God's love for you and the truth of our desire to sin?

3. Are you a dry drunk? What are you denying yourself that you secretly crave?

4. What fruit do you bear?

5. How can we help others, and ourselves, to admit our sins?

6. How can we help others, and ourselves, to realize that we can't fix ourselves?

7. How can we help others, and ourselves, to embrace our constraints?

8. How can you remember that you are set apart?

Chapter 7

BE LOVING

Among the people who hated us when we (Timothy) were starting Leaders School at Raranya was Mr. Christopher. This person did not even want the school to be started there. However, when we started, we took his daughter Catherine and sponsored her. Catherine now is in Class III. Christopher and his wife are now one of the best friends of Leaders School. All the time they want to give advice or offer to us things like chicken, cooked maize, or flour, according to what they can afford. They have become a blessing to us.

Hatred comes from the devil. It is the spirit that works to separate people and create enmity. On top of that, hatred makes the person who holds it to become the slave of the devil. In the end, the devil rejoices when two people fight to the point of killing one another.

Glory be to God—among the advantages of accepting Christ to be your Savior and Master is how He transforms your DNA by instilling His immeasurable love into your inner system, which triggers you to enjoy loving people.

I can't forget one day, when a certain poor family slaughtered a fat grown-up turkey that they liked most. They just wanted to surprise their neighbors and show them love. Their neighbor was of a middle-class level. By coincidence, that same day the husband and wife had been fighting, so nothing was prepared for dinner. Without knowing, the poor family took their well-cooked turkey and rice to their neighbors and knocked on the door. Filled with joy and shouts, they entered the house and told their neighbors they wanted to surprise them with fellowship, and by eating together the turkey that was known to almost every neighbor.

From that time, the atmosphere changed in that house. The husband and wife came together; the two children in the house became happy; and without knowing, the neighbors discussed their marriage and relationship and how they felt about having such good neighbors. By the time they finished eating and talking, the husband stood up and talked about what had happened before they entered. Instead of putting it as a case, the husband narrated it as a lesson God wanted them to learn. He apologized and hugged his wife. And on the following Sunday, they went to their neighbor's church for Sunday service and gave their lives to Christ.

Love is Christ's heart. One of the indicators that we have Christ in us is having a passion for loving others, loving our neighbors, even loving our enemies.

Ambassadors love their enemies and
their neighbors.

Love Your Enemies

But I tell you, love your enemies and pray for those who persecute you.

(Matthew 5:44)

The Lord's Prayer says it clearly: "And forgive us our debts, as we also have forgiven our debtors" (Matthew 6:12). We are not to hold on to our grudges. We are to let them go so that we will be forgiven. If we are to be part of God's family, we need to genuinely love one another, despite hurtful acts on the part of other people. "Lord, how many times shall I forgive my brother when he sins against me?" Peter asked Christ. "Up to seven times?" Jesus answered, "I tell you, not seven times, but seventy times seven" (Matthew 18:21–22).

Jesus goes on to describe the kingdom of heaven being like a king who wanted to settle accounts with his servant. There was one servant who owed him ten thousand talents (Matthew 18:23–35). That's an incredible amount of money, since King Herod had a yearly income of only nine hundred talents and Galilee and Peraea (the land beyond the Jordan) in the year 4 BC brought in just two hundred talents in taxes. This servant owed the king more money than he could possibly repay, and he and his family were to be sold into slavery.

The servant pleaded with the king to be patient with him and was later pardoned of his debt in an act of mercy. This same servant was then found choking a fellow servant who owed him one hundred denari (a day's wages), demanding payment. When the king heard of the behavior of the just-pardoned servant, he was furious and had him thrown into jail to be tortured until he should pay back all that he owed. The parable ends with Jesus warning, "This is how my heavenly Father will treat each of you unless you forgive your brother from your heart" (v. 35).

These are clear instructions. A sin is an incalculable offense against God, but we are released from its burden by the atoning sacrifice that Jesus made. Remembering His forgiving grace, we are commanded to go out and love others.

And yet, we often have trouble following through on this command and often find ourselves holding grudges for a long time. Part of the reason is that we tend to rationalize why people do what they do, especially when they do it repeatedly. In trying to understand the reasons for their behavior, we often imagine motives that are convenient and usually not very true. We are more apt to imagine an orchestrated plot against us instead of an act of negligence, ignoring the reality that all of us are broken in some way. We too quickly forgive ourselves of our own short-comings while holding the other person to a higher standard. And, unfortunately, we commit these errors over and over.

Being Christian means that we must take up our cross and deny ourselves. Denying one's self means that forgiveness is not based on our ability to punish the transgressor to a similar degree. Nor does it mean that we forgive the other person if we can get back what was taken from us. It does not mean that we forgive because other people put pressure on us so that we can all get along. Instead, taking up one's cross means that we forgive because we are called to love the other person as Jesus loved us, and that a hurtful act on their part does not alter that sense of love.

Men occasionally ask us (Greg) to help them in out in terms of lending them money during their stay. In the early part of our ministry we didn't see anything wrong with this, but as time has gone by, we are reluctant to get involved in men's lives in this way. The reason for borrowing the money always sounds good to begin with but almost never ends up being a good idea. A man may want to get a car, or may have trouble moving to a particular part of town so that they are near family, and our heart goes out to them because we've gotten to know them and they've become like family to us.

However, lending money then not having it paid back can be a curse to everyone involved. The man receiving the money carries the guilt of an unpaid debt with them and this hinders any relationship that ensues. It also hinders my ability to love because I start wondering why in the world this man would not attempt to pay back even some of his debt, or even acknowledge it periodically. The reasons, of course, are unknown to me; as a Christian I'm called to love, despite feeling like I've been abused.

A difficult aspect of ministering to the needy is figuring out where to set boundaries. People who don't have money will naturally want your (or anybody's) money, and if this drive is coupled with not having a good idea of what an acceptable request looks like, there are bound to be hurt feelings. We have found that many people will resent the fact that you have money, despite the hard work that went into obtaining it. Some of the men we have ministered to felt that it was all right to steal from us because we had enough money anyway. I suspect this is one of the reasons that churches may be segregated by income—it's difficult to go to church to worship with the feeling that you're the source of envy or hate about being privileged.

But the fact of the matter is, Christians are called to be cheerful givers. Much is expected of individuals to whom much is given. I didn't pick my parents, didn't pick my family, and didn't pick the neighborhood where I grew up or the high school that I attended. I'm not even responsible for my election. So what am I so worried about? My worth to God as an ambassador is directly related to how far out I set my boundaries of charity and love. We are called to be discerning in our service to others and ask God for wisdom in our response to their needs and requests, not short-circuiting the spiritual formation that takes place as a man struggles with God. So, we pray about how best to love.

Forgiving . . . to Be Blessed

We all would like forgiveness,
    for the things that we've done wrong
And for harboring resentments . . .
    which may be very strong

But it isn't always easy,
    and I'm sure we'll all agree
That until you show forgiveness . . .
    you cannot be really free

Don't we all know someone . . .
    who rubbed our angry nerve?
Who upset us or disgusted us
    by pitching us a curve?

And haven't we all told someone,
    "I forgive you . . . it's okay"
Just because we thought it was
    proper thing to say?

When asked if we are still upset,
    we sometimes tell a lie
We don't like to admit it,
    but you've done it . . . so have I

Inside we feel that churning
    as they're walking through the door
We choose not to forgive them,
    but that's not who it's for

We are the ones who benefit
    by choosing to forgive
By lining up with the Word of God
    we learn again to live

To live without the bitterness
    and the anger that we face
To live without those feelings
    that we try hard to erase

We struggle with forgiveness,
    for we can't forgive with ease
Even when the person asks,
    "Will you forgive me, please?"

We need to be forgiven, too,
    in far more ways than one
And the shoe is on the other foot
    considering what we've done

Our God forgives each one of us
    according to His Word
We only need to ask Him . . .
    I'm sure that you have heard

God forgives completely
     and He doesn't make a fuss
But according to how we forgive
     those who anger us

Forgiving makes us stronger
     which will help us in a bind
It also is the measurement
     that we must keep in mind

Go ahead and feel the anger . . .
     or the negative attitude
But remember God forgives you,
     so show Him gratitude

God will often lean on us
     to step up to the plate
To forgive and ask forgiveness,
     before it is too late

Please don't put forgiveness off;
     it could be just a test
God may want to know
     if you are ready to be blessed

Love Your Neighbor

*And the second is like it: "Love your neighbor
as yourself."*

(Matthew 22:39)

I (Greg) met Benjamin Graham four days after he was released from prison at a breakfast ministry in downtown Columbus, Ohio. I sat down across from him and asked how his week had gone. He told me that he was just released from prison, and that among other things he was a poet. I asked if I could see some of his poetry, expecting to read something not so great while searching for words of encouragement and expression that might need to be said.

I was amazed as I read the first poem, and then another. I told him that he needed to get his poetry published, and remember poking him in the chest as I said it. It was from this encounter that a newsletter was born and our friendship began. Of all the people I have met at that downtown church, he is the person with whom I am most spiritually aligned. It was in God's plan for us to meet, and it is God's plan for us to continue our ministry together through the newsletter and to our transition houses for men coming out of prison.

I am not sure how I know this, but I do know it. There are things that ring true in our lives, and things that each of us rely on to guide us in our walk with God. The apostle Peter provides us with some practical markers for knowing whether we are part of God's plan as he writes:

> For this very reason, make every effort to add to your faith goodness; and to goodness, knowledge; and to knowledge, self-control; and to self-control, perseverance; and to perseverance, godliness; and to godliness, brotherly kindness; and to brotherly kindness, love. (2 Peter 1:5–7, NIV1984)

I may not know if some of the specific steps I take in my walk are the right ones, but I learn from this passage where I am headed. My walk with God begins when I have faith in Him, and is destined to bring me to the greatest human virtue, love. The progression described above provides me with checkpoints that I can use to make sure that I am on course.

It starts with faith; "without faith it is impossible to please God" (Hebrews 11:6). From faith we progress to goodness, where our actions are done out of our love and desire to know Him better. We do this by reading the Bible, testing and approving what God tells us in Scripture (Romans 12:2). The Bible is God's Word for His people. The Bible doesn't make much sense to people who don't want to know God—people who don't admit there is a Holy Creator who is the Author of our lives (1 Corinthians 1:18). God reveals the meaning of Scripture to people who seek Him, and clouds its meaning from those who do not.

It is by reading the Bible that we learn about God and His holiness. God hates sin, and as we desire to draw closer to God, we come to realize that we need to stop turning our backs on God. We start to develop self-control out of our love for Him, and God helps us in our walk by giving us opportunities to refine and deepen our ability to persevere through hardship. Hardships are no longer thought of in a negative way; instead we actually begin to look forward to them as we find that our sufferings will produce perseverance, and our perseverance, character (Romans 5:4)—the kind of character described in Jesus' Sermon on the Mount. Christians are people who are poor in spirit, mourn, are meek and who thirst for righteousness. They are people who are merciful, pure in heart, peacemakers, and persecuted (Matthew 5:1–12). As we move along this progression, our character becomes more godly and we are able to express brotherly kindness and love.

I am convinced that all of us can love as we carry out God's work in this world. Hands can love, feet can love, and elbows can love. We shouldn't worry about which part of the body of Christ we function as; we should just strive to love as we do our job. My meeting Benjamin was no coincidence. As we continue our work, I hope to learn to love more deeply and broadly than I do now.

Love is the reason that men turn toward God. They begin to have hope for something better than they have today and develop a willingness to participate in God's kingdom. Some men don't stay on the uphill path to improvement because they don't have a clear idea of the direction they are heading. There may not have been tangible expressions of goodness, knowledge, self-control, perseverance, or brotherly kindness in their lives. Or, they may be so depressed and disgusted with themselves that they don't know how to pull themselves out of the pit they've gotten themselves into. Having hope gives men the resources to march uphill along the ladder of sanctification described in 2 Peter 1:5–7.

Last summer Timothy and Happiness Wambura visited us from Tanzania. They stayed with us for a week and became part of our lives. We love hearing their impressions of the work we are doing in Columbus, and they also love to hear about what we think as we see what they are doing in Africa. Timothy observed that the men in our houses were in need of a place to worship. When I pursued this with the men, I found that none of them felt comfortable in churches that they visited after being released, because they sensed that they weren't really welcomed. Their presence was tolerated, but they were sometimes asked to sit in a special section, or they noticed that people moved their children and their purses a little closer to themselves when they were near.

We decided to look into having a church service especially designed for people who have been to prison. My wife and I asked the pastor of the church across the street from the Fort Jackson house, and he was agreeable to it. We then went to the parole board in Columbus and they also were open to it. When the men heard about the possibility of having their own church, they were extremely open to it. So, we started organizing for church.

We decided to call it "Second Chance Church" and picked Isaiah 61:1 as our seed verse:

> The Spirit of the Sovereign Lord is on me,
>
> because the Lord has anointed me
>
> to proclaim good news to the poor.
>
> He has sent me to bind up the brokenhearted,
>
> to proclaim freedom for the captives
>
> and release from darkness for the prisoners.

We also developed a tagline:

Second Chance Church

Freedom for Captives

We then started to think about who would do the preaching, whether or not we would have a band, how we would organize a website, who would be greeters, and who might want to give their testimonies. As the list of things we needed to get done grew, excitement grew along with it. The men in the houses, as well as men who used to be in the houses, wanted to participate in some way.

The idea of having their own "church" gave men hope. It gave them a reason to want to be good and be part of something bigger than themselves. It provided a tangible expression of how they could do good. Men who were despondent and somewhat depressed perked up and began putting their skills to use for God. They knew they belonged, and they wanted to love.

God Is in Control

There will never be another you . . .
    and not another me

Each of us come from a different mold,
    and we won't all agree

We each may come from a different world . . .
    from the other side of town

Perhaps with different views on life
    (up and sometimes down)

But when haphazardly we meet,
    as often is the case

And find a growing friendship
    right before us, taking place

When alignment of the spirit forms
    a bond we can't deny

We know it is God's intention;
    there's no other reason why

So we must then embrace these friendships,
    watching as they grow

Allowing God to lead . . .
    for only He knows where they'll go.

Discussion Questions

1. What grudges do you hold on to?

2. How do you play offense in God's kingdom?

3. What boundaries do you need to set to protect yourself as you love? How can these boundaries be relaxed?

4. Do you always give cheerfully? When is it hardest to do this?

5. Who claims you as his neighbor?

6. Where are you on the ladder of sanctification described in 2 Peter 1:5–7? What next step on the ladder do you need to take?

7. Why is it that people tend to forget what they've been given when it's time for them to give?

8. How can you provide a safe place where others can express their love?

Chapter 8

BE GENEROUS

Being generous is where God is needed most. It needs God's guidance when it comes to be a godly generous person otherwise it might be just wasting resources. This is the area that fights selfishness, rudeness, discourtesy, and the like.

Godly generosity is very different from just being generous. Godly generosity comes when a person hears and adheres to God's voice inside him and he does that for God's glory and honor. By doing that the Bible puts it very clear that you are saving in your heavenly account. Being generous is being faithful to God by giving out what He has deposited in you. God wants people to know that what they hold is not theirs but His. He wants His people to be connected to others by being generous. He wants people to be connected to Him by becoming His giving agents. That's why when a person gives rightly, he gets a feeling that he has given to God. God calls us to be generous.

Ambassadors are generous.

For where your treasure is, there your heart will be also.

(Matthew 6:21)

Generosity requires our heart. The condition of our heart is so important that it is mentioned more than five hundred times in the Bible. From Genesis to Revelation, it defines our relationship with God and our relationship with each other. Our faith is made complete through the heart, and we pray that what is on our heart, in our heart, and what passes through our heart is found pleasing to God.

God will look into all of our hearts on judgment day. Paul writes in his letter to the Romans, concerning the Gentiles who do not live under the law or know the commands of God:

> Indeed, when Gentiles ... do by nature things required by the law, they ... show that the requirements of the law are written on their hearts, their consciences also bearing witness, and their thoughts sometimes accusing them and at other time even defending them. (Romans 2:14–16)

Our salvation comes from declaring with our mouth that "Jesus is Lord," and believing in our heart that God raised Him from the dead (Romans 10:9). It is much more than just having Bible knowledge. People of faith have experienced a change of heart that causes them to want to serve genuinely and give generously. They accept the call of being part of God's family, wanting to conform themselves to family expectations and uphold family values.

God is generous and His ambassadors are called to be generous. Think of the amount of unused space present in the

universe, the number of acorns that fall from an oak tree, or
the number of times God invited us into His family before we
accepted His invitation. There is abundant evidence of His generosity in providing for us and being patient with us. We are
called to do the same and witness without restraint as we reach
out to others (Matthew 13:1–9). Only God knows what is, or
what will be, in a person's heart.

My children played soccer when they were young, and I was
one of their coaches. It didn't seem to bother the rest of the
parents that I had never actually played soccer in my youth.
My sport was basketball. But I figured that there are common
things to all sports, and if I could teach the kids things like
holding their position on the field, not to chase the ball, and
to keep their heads up, then they would play well. And, if the
kids were attentive enough and I was fortunate enough, I could
teach them the secret weapon of all youth sports—the give-and-
go play, where one player passes the ball to their teammate and
hopes that the defender follows the ball instead of them while
they sprint to the goal for a pass and a score. If I could teach
them that, I was sure we'd win the championship.

One of the hardest things about coaching youth sports is
figuring out which position each child would play. My hope
was that I could allow them to explore each position—forward,
midfield, and backfield—and try to get them to see what they
wanted to play. This was a great plan, but was a disaster to imple-
ment. Some kids literally can't run, and others are so distracted
that putting them on defense is just an invitation for the other
team to score a goal. One of the positions I was sensitive to not
letting everyone try was goalie, unless we were winning by a
lot (which we never were). This was a position that I needed to
have someone I could rely on as the last line of defense. Youth

players don't have much of a leg, and so there aren't really any scores from far away from the goal; a good goalie was worth their weight in gold.

In about my third year of coaching, one of the slower, more passive players on the team decided that he wanted to play goalie. This child rarely ran for more than ten yards without being completely winded. When he did manage to get himself near the ball, he would rarely kick it. He seemed to prefer chasing after the opposing players than challenging them. If I had to grade the players on the team on their ability to play goalie, he would have been near the bottom of the list.

What makes a good soccer player a great soccer player? The same thing that makes a good math teacher a great math teacher and a good musician a great musician—heart. Heart transforms the learning in the head—e.g., the rules of the game, the rules of algebra, or the rules of music—into something owned and expressed by the person. A person's heart transforms something external to something internal so that it becomes part of them.

My passive player eventually was given the chance to play goalie, and his transformation was amazing. He quickly learned how to defend his goal and was aggressive in doing it. He saved many balls from scoring, and grew to become a dependable player. This is something that I would not have predicted. He played his position with heart.

Faith works the same way. People can read the Bible, learn about God in the Old Testament, the life and work of Jesus in the Gospels, and acts of the Holy Spirit in the Epistles, but never bring this into their hearts until the day they experience saving faith. Saving faith involves the movement of what's in one's head into one's heart. Faith is made real when it becomes personal, and it eventually drives a person to act out their faith, to become the hands and feet of Christ, in some tangible way. Head, heart, and hands will show the marks of deep faith.

One of the greatest joys we have in our ministry is when a man comes back to us. Men almost always start out great and are so thankful for not being in prison anymore. But their enthusiasm doesn't last unless they are committed to changing their ways. Some of the men quickly start to shortcut their duties and try to navigate a dual lifestyle with one foot in the ministry and another in the world. This strategy doesn't work because you can't do both, and the alternative life shows itself in a few weeks. Other men take longer and stay on the path until they are confronted with a real choice involving sacrifice. This often occurs when they get a car and have a paycheck. When men go off the path and leave the ministry, we almost always tell them that they can come back to us if they want. They can always attend Bible study on Tuesday nights, and we're happy to give them some clothes and a shower if they need them. God didn't give up on us, and we have no desire of giving up on them.

It's All about the Heart

If no one would know and no one could tell,
what list of things would you do?
Where would you go and how would you act
if no one could see it but you?

If there were no repercussions,
and no consequences to pay
How many deviant actions
would you do throughout the day?

By nature we're creatures of pleasure,
we love what makes us feel good
Even the things we know to be wrong,
we do much more that we should (Romans 7:18–19)

No one at all is excluded . . .
we all fall short of perfection
The good, the bad, the rich, the poor . . .
each of us need some correction

No one can know what you're thinking . . .
no one on earth is so smart
But God knows all of your secrets,
for God looks at the heart (1 Samuel 16:7)

Can you honestly say you're proud
of the way that others hear you speak?
Do you go to church on Sundays,
and cuss all through the week?

When people lie and cheat and steal
and do bad things to you
Does your flesh kick in before you can ask . . .
"What would Jesus do?"

Have you looked at sexy people . . .
and wished you had the chance
To spend some time alone with them
to see what's in their . . . refrigerator?

These things come from the heart, my friends,
and it's wicked beyond measure
Under the surface, there is our heart . . .
embracing the things we treasure (Luke 12:34)

There is no darkness, or hidden thoughts . . .
no hiding place for you
God's eyes are on the ways of man,
seeing everything you do (Job 34:21–22)

God is not surprised at us;
He knew right from the start
That we could not obey His laws
(even hidden in our heart) (Psalm 119:11)

So all of us should take some time
to check our heart's condition
And spend more time in the Word of God
to boost our heart's nutrition

Let's pay attention to what we say
and examine how we act
Let's practice being Christians,
until it becomes a fact

Let's pray and ask God to help us,
to live out better days
Let's stop and take a look inside
and consider all our ways (Haggai 1:5)

Let us scrutinize our thoughts my friends,
and now is the time to start
Let us realize our walk with God
is all about the heart.

A man came to us after serving fifteen years for a man-slaughter charge. He was from the South and was very lovable. He would often say, "Hello, my name is—and I'd appreciate your vote for mayor." He was uplifting, encouraging, and spent his time in the Bible and helping others. This man conformed to the house rules, didn't break curfew, and was genuinely a nice guy. In about the sixth month of his stay with us, he began looking for a car; at that same time, another man approached me at church saying he wanted to bless our ministry. I immediately thought of this man and suggested that he could use a car. This suggestion was well received, as the man from church had a brother who was restoring a car in Pennsylvania at that time.

The man from church drove to Pennsylvania to get the car, and then we had to change the title to get Ohio tags. So we all met at the Bureau of Motor Vehicles to sign things over, and the man from church got to meet the man receiving the vehicle. At one point that morning, when the man receiving the car was waiting in line, the man from church pulled me aside and asked, "What crime did he commit?" This is something we usually don't worry about much in our ministry because we believe that when men come to Christ, they are a new creation (2 Corinthians 5:17). I looked the man up on the internet and saw that it was a manslaughter charge; the man from church didn't say too much.

The car was beautiful, it ran great, and the tires were good. Unfortunately, the man who received the car used it to do more than just go back and forth to work. He started to show up to work late, eventually lost his job, and from we could tell was no longer on the path. He moved out of the house and requested his savings a little at a time, but was spending through the money at a fast rate.

During this time, the man from church would ask about the man who got the car, and I would keep him abreast of what was going on. The man from church had a great attitude throughout this ordeal and did not feel that anything was wasted or that he had been cheated. He believed that he did what God asked him to do, and that the rest was not his responsibility. The man from church continued to pray for the man with the car.

Many people want to know the outcome of their efforts before engaging in a generous act. They recoil at the thought of giving money to a beggar at a freeway exit ramp or in a parking lot because they might not use it for buying food. The idea of giving someone money, and then them using it to buy a six-pack of beer, is repulsive. So they go through life tight-fisted with their time, money, and emotions and want to know if a charity is "worthy" of their resources. The same mindset was present in all of us before we came to saving faith—we wanted God to tell us His plan before we would decide whether we would commit to Him. But that is not how faith works. We don't believe in God because of what He will do for us. We believe God because He is God, and we do what God tells us to do for the same reason.

The man with the car eventually spent through all of his money, and then enrolled in a recovery program at the Salvation Army. He is there today as he tries to get his life back together, and we are storing his car at the ministry house until he completes his program. We take great joy in welcoming back to our ministry the men who have had to "go around the mountain" another time. Benjamin, the house manager at Covenant House, had to go around the mountain many times before he finally saw the light and was able to change his life. His compassion and generosity make him a perfect house manager and an ambassador of Heaven.

Generosity requires the head and the heart to work together. It requires a heart for others, as well as the ability to "pick up your head" in the middle of a spiritual battle and remember that the enemy is not the person giving us trouble, but the spirit in the person leading him in the wrong direction. I used to tell my soccer players to "pick up their heads" so they could see the game and anticipate where the ball might go next. Ambassadors need to do the same, so that they don't get frustrated with outcomes that might take longer than expected.

The Condition of Your Heart

The condition of your heart reflects
    the man who lives within
Doing things half-heartedly
    is no way to begin

Whatever you may do in life . . .
    step up to the plate
Put your heart into it. . . .
    It's what will make you great

Teachers know it, coaches know it,
    and surely you do, too
It's best to get your heart involved
    in everything you do

Pretending that your heart is in it . . .
    doesn't work for long
Especially when it comes to God,
    who knows when we are wrong

From the righteous conversations
    and the "oh so holy" look
To memorizing scriptures
    from within the Holy Book

We may deceive our fellowman,
    claiming to be smart
But we cannot fool the Master . . .
    who looks into the heart

Appearing to be righteous
    many claim to have no sin
But we would be surprised
    if we could only see "within"

The condition of the heart is
    mentioned all throughout the Bible
But looking at the outer man
    is very unreliable

It's there within your heart
    where you must cease to be a sinner
From ordinary "outside"
    to extraordinary "inner"

God indeed looks on the heart . . .
    the language there is true
It's who we really are . . .
    and what we really wish to do

Knowing what the scriptures say
    is simply not enough
We must experience "saving faith,"
    and yes, this can be tough

If we are truly born again . . .
    the flesh can now be dead
As we transfer to the heart . . .
    all the truth that's in our head

Christ died and rose again for us
    if only we'll receive it
We must confess it with our mouth,
    and in our heart . . . believe it

Speaking of our righteousness
    to give ourselves a "toast"
And bragging of our faithfulness
    as if there's room to boast

We keep our flesh alive
    while our spirit is asleep
We talk about how good we are,
    forgetting "talk is cheap"

Bearing witness in our heart
    dispels the useless chatter
The condition of the heart *is*
    . . . the heart of the matter

Discussion Questions

1. What do you treasure?

2. When God looks at your heart, what does He see?

3. What is stuck in your head that needs to get into your heart?

4. What do others see when they consider your heart? Does your checkbook and appointment calendar support this point of view?

5. Do you lead with your head, your heart, or your hands? How do you get the other parts involved?

6. Why do you think that people's heads and hearts are often in conflict?

7. Think of a time when you were exceptionally generous, and talk about how your heart was touched.

8. How can you help people more fully engage their hearts?

Chapter 9

BE FAITHFUL

One day when I (Timothy) was working in Mwanza, one of the cities in Tanzania, I was in Barclays Bank. One of the cashiers from one of the municipal councils came to withdraw a big amount of cash money for staff salary. Unfortunately, when he packed the bags in a big cash box under police escort, he forgot one bag and went off heading to Geita, about 120 kilometers from Mwanza. At that time, there were no mobile phones. Back in the bank, the cashier reported the incident to his supervisor, and that reached up to the bank branch manager; the money was kept intact in the safe.

When the district office cashier reached his office and started to count up the money, together with the police who escorted him, he realized there was a shortage of one bag of money. Without telling anyone in the office, they drove immediately back to Mwanza. The bank was closed, but the staff were still inside finalizing their day's work. The police knocked on the back door and it was opened for them; the moment that bank cashier saw them, he went and told the branch manager. They were given their money intact.

The news spread, and when it became known to the higher authorities, the branch manager and the cashier were both promoted for their faithfulness. I knew this because the cashier was my neighbor and a friend. I always tell people that faithfulness to God and His people is a big capital one can have. It is not only God who looks for a faithful person, but even human beings do so. What employers look for most in the people they employ is faithfulness.

> Ambassadors are faithful.

Therefore what God has joined together, let no one separate.

(Matthew 19:6)

My (Greg's) wife sometimes calls to me from another room and expects me to understand what she is saying. It sounds like mumbling from where I'm sitting, and it bothers me to not know what she is saying. Even worse, when I say, "What?" nothing happens. There is just silence. I may get up, go to her, and ask her to repeat herself. It is only then that I can understand what is on her mind and respond in some reasonable way.

Understanding the reason behind things is important to me. It helps me see the bigger picture. Once I know why something needs to be done, I can better participate in the solution and react to unexpected things that arise. All of us want to better understand what is desired and expected of us.

The Old Testament book of Job is about a righteous man who suffers cruelly. God allows Job to be tested by Satan, and in the process of these tests Job loses his livestock, his family, and suffers terrible sickness. Three friends visit Job through these trials, who try to comfort him and offer reasons for his bad fortune. Surely, they say, there must be something Job has done to cause these calamities. "Who, being innocent, has ever perished?" (Job 4:7), they ask. But Job insists that he has done nothing wrong. "Does God pervert justice?" asks another friend, suggesting that Job "seek God earnestly and plead with the Almighty" (Job 8:3, 5). But Job at first resists this suggestion, knowing that he is unworthy of disputing with God. Eventually, though, Job does seek out God to "argue [his] case" (Job 13:3). In other words, Job's suffering eventually brings him to question God's ways.

God says to Job:

> Brace yourself like a man; I will question you, and you shall answer me. Where were you when I laid the earth's foundation? Tell me, if you understand. Who marked off its dimensions? Surely you know! Who shut up the sea behind doors when it burst forth from the womb, when I made the clouds its garment[?] . . . Have you ever given orders to the morning, or shown the dawn its place[?] . . . Have you entered the storehouses of the snow, or seen the storehouses of the hail[?] (Job 38:3–9, 12, 22)

Upon hearing this, Job realizes his transgression against God and admits, "Surely I spoke of things I did not understand, things too wonderful for me to know" (Job 42:3). God's ways are higher than our ways. We, like Job, are called to fear God, trust Him, love Him, and know Him, but it's impossible for us to understand Him. How can we possibly understand God's plans? Yet, this question is almost always raised by people who resist God. They want to know "the plan" before they will agree to love Him with all their heart.

God asks Job, "Would you condemn me to justify yourself?" (Job 40:8b). This question has great implications of how we all relate to God. It is the question of every person who resists God's Word, claiming that society has moved beyond the teachings of the Bible and the rejection of behavior once described as sinful. It is present in churches and movements emphasizing one portion of the Bible while rejecting others. It is seen in every attempt to make the Bible applicable to everyday life instead of making everyday life applicable to the wisdom and truth of God's Word.

Suffering is not always because we sin, but in the process of suffering we often sin because we get angry with God. We should never blame God, as Job did in arguing his case, because God never makes mistakes. We need to trust that God will use our suffering to teach us and refine us, so that we may see Him more clearly.

Trying to understand God is foolish and only leads to worry. God does not want us to worry. When He wants us to do something, He will let us know. In the meantime, spend your time preparing for a godly assignment by fearing, trusting, loving, and knowing Him as He is revealed in Scripture.

Men coming out of prison worry a lot. They worry about how they will fit back into society, whether they will find a good job and how people will react to knowing that they've been to prison. It's easy to forget about God when we are focused entirely on ourselves. Yet, God has brought everyone through trials and

His presence is made evident to us in many ways. Remembering to remember God is sometimes difficult.

One day the house manager at Fort Jackson said that the house needed an Ebenezer. An Ebenezer was erected by Samuel in a battle against the Philistines at a time of Israel's history where they tried to manage God and use Him in battle. The Israelites realized their transgression after the ark of the covenant was captured, and Samuel brought the nation back into repentance. As the Israelites were worshipping God in Mizpah, the Philistines were gathering to attack, but God intervened, and the Philistines were routed.

> Then Samuel took a stone and set it up between Mizpah and Shen. He named it Ebenezer, saying, "Thus far the Lord has helped us." (1 Samuel 7:12)

I thought that erecting a stone of help was a great idea to help remind our men of God's presence in their lives. We traveled down to a quarry located on the south side of Columbus and asked to see their biggest boulder. They had a six-ton granite rock that was available for $3,000, and I didn't blink when they asked if I wanted it. It was so cool.

A dump truck was used to place it on the Fort Jackson property, and when it hit the ground one morning, no one was going to move it ever again. The earth literally shook, and the boulder created an indentation in the ground. I was excited because everyone traveling along the highway next to the house would see it, and when asked we could tell people it was our "stone of help."

I went home after the delivery and my wife asked where I had been that morning. I had forgotten to tell her about our plans and going down to the quarry on the south side. Eventually the conversation came around to how much it cost, and she said, "You paid $3,000 for a rock?" I tried to tell her it wasn't just a rock; it was an Ebenezer! She wasn't buying the story and I went into work feeling a little low.

I got to work at noon, and at about 1 p.m. the dean of my college came into my office. He said that he had heard about my work with men coming out of prison, and handed me a check for more than the price of the rock. I thought God's timing was impeccable. Not only was I out of the doghouse at home, but I actually ended up with more money than I originally paid. I brought the check home that evening and showed it to my wife, who said, "I guess it *was* an Ebenezer."

Brian, the former house manager at Fort Jackson, is a wonderful example of a faithful servant. He became the manager during a difficult time in his marriage when he and his wife had separated. I was thankful to have a Lion of God managing Fort Jackson, but felt bad for him as he struggled in his marriage. He was the house manager for about four years. During this period, he would sometimes become discouraged and angry, but I never heard him utter one bad word against his situation. He continued to have faith and was patient, knowing God was in charge. The thaw in their relationship came after much prayer and patience, and he left Fort Jackson to be with her again. I miss him in the ministry, but I'm so thankful for his powerful witness and dedication to God.

Just Be Still and Listen

Why is it so difficult
    for us to stop and chill
Why is it that we move so much
    when God says, "Just be still"?

Ripping, running blindly through
    this world that's full of strife
When we could learn from nature;
    being still may save our life

We know that God is for us;
    He has proven it before
No one can come and harm us . . .
    for He's standing at the door

Stay among the flock
    instead of always on the go
Jesus is our shepherd . . .
    our Good Shepherd, don't you know?

There's no need to hide
    when the enemy makes a threat
God said He'd fight our battles . . .
    and He hasn't failed us yet

Do we not hear Him speaking . . .
    when He tells us not to fear?
Or perhaps we're just too busy . . .
    to give a listening ear

Too busy being worried . . .
      about our "Jezebel"
She's seeking to destroy us . . .
      so we put ourselves through hell

Looking over our shoulder . . .
      and ducking down in fear
Winding up in caves wondering
      "How did I get here?"

But, just like with Elijah . . .
      our God will intercede
He's our "very present help" . . .
      whenever we have need

He cares about us, big time . . .
      to Him we're never "petty"
To get us through our trouble spots
      He's always there and ready

Why? Because He loves us . . .
      and for us He has a plan
It doesn't matter where you are;
      He wants to use your hand

Stop running, settle down . . .
      you don't know what you're missin'
God is trying to talk to you . . .
      just be still and listen

Discussion Questions

1. Is there anything about God—His purpose, His timing, His plan, anything—that you question? What is it?

2. What is it about yourself that you tend to self-justify?

3. What do you tend to worry about?

4. Name an Ebenezer in your life that helps you remember that, "Thus far the LORD has helped us."

5. Name something in your life to which you have remained faithful.

6. To what do you want to remain faithful going forward?

7. Why is it hard for you to just be still and listen?

8. How can we help others to remember what God has done for them?

Chapter 10

BE A ROLE MODEL

One of the things that has made our (Timothy's) Leaders School in Raranya favored is how the children, who formerly were problematic in terms of their character and behavior in their families and the community, have been changed by Christ and become good examples in their families and up to the neighboring Raranya Government Primary School and Raranya Secondary School. The feedback we get from the neighboring schools is that teachers, as they correct their schoolchildren, use Leaders School children as good examples of how the children are supposed to behave.

We know it is by God's grace that the children who join us find Leaders School to be a place where the presence of Jesus Christ and the movement of the Holy Spirit is so vivid, personal, and powerful. Leaders School normally enrolls children the way they are, trusting that God will change them to be the way He wants them to be. And that's what happens, often without too much of a struggle. The call of Jesus is true and amen, saying, "Come to me, all you who are weary and burdened, and I will give you rest" (Matthew 11:28). We see our Leaders School children, teachers, and staff enjoying the rest that Jesus gives.

We are committed at the Leaders School Raranya to raise a new generation of people who are saturated in Christ, and to provide a high-quality education that will enable them to impact the world. We want to see our schoolchildren, teachers, and staff have lives that reflect heavenly citizenship by their words and deeds.

Every nation has canons of ethics for her citizens. We always ask God to help us make the Leaders School an island of its own where people can learn and live heavenly citizenship—a place where God is the center of everything, a place where God is revered and worshipped.

The truth of the matter is, if it were not for the downfall of human beings, our lives would reflect good heavenly citizenship. We were robbed of this very valuable and noble possession, the character of heaven. However, we thank God He worked on that through the death of His begotten Son Jesus Christ, and that our valuable heavenly citizenship can be restored by accepting Jesus Christ as personal Savior and Master.

> Ambassadors set good examples and
> are good citizens.

Be a Good Example

You are the light of the world. A town built on a hill cannot be hidden.

(Matthew 5:14)

One of my favorite passages in the Bible is the story of Paul and Silas. These two men were stripped, beaten, flogged, and thrown into prison for expelling a spirit in a slave girl (Acts 16:16–40). The spirit allowed her to tell fortunes, and the owners realized that their money-making days were over when the spirit departed. The owners accused Paul and Silas of promoting customs that were unlawful to Romans practice. The jailer put Paul and Silas in a secure cell and fastened their feet in the stocks.

> About midnight Paul and Silas were praying and singing hymns to God, and the other prisoners were listening to them. (Acts 16:25)

What I love about this passage is that Paul and Silas don't try to stand up for their rights. The slave girl had been following the two men around for many days, shouting, "These men are servants of the Most High God, who are telling you the way to be saved" (v. 17). Paul became so annoyed with her that he turned around and said to the spirit, "In the name of Jesus Christ I command you to come out of her!" (v. 18). At that moment the spirit left her, and then the trouble began.

Paul and Silas accepted that they were in jail and made the most of their situation. They didn't focus on the fact that the charges were trumped up or that the slaveowners were being vindictive. They didn't stew about being treated unfairly and didn't demand a retrial. All that we know is that they sang hymns and prayed that night, and that other prisoners were listening to them. In other words, they witnessed.

I think about this passage when I'm in a tough situation. I know that being a Christian doesn't deliver me from tough times, but instead it is in tough times that I am delivered.

> Not only so, but we also glory in our sufferings, because we know that suffering produces perseverance; perseverance, character; and character, hope. And hope does not put us to shame, because God's love has been poured out into our hearts through the Holy Spirit, who has been given to us. (Romans 5:3–5)

It is one thing to know that I should welcome tough times because they encourage me to draw closer to God and develop my character. But it is another thing to know how to act in these moments. The actions of Paul and Silas show me how to move forward and not look back, not saying "but," and not hoping for a different today. The past is past, the future is for tomorrow, and I am called to respond to the conditions of my "today."

One of the things that I've come to believe in working with men coming out of prison is that God is the God of all things, however small. We see miracles occur on a weekly basis—such as a man getting a call from a relative, a job becoming available, or an opportunity arising at just the right time. There is just no explaining these events without believing that God's hand is present. God brings us to difficult situations to teach us something. We may not know what that something is, but God does.

We are all called to be set apart for the gospel. We do this in words, actions, and by the character we express as we go through difficult times. The great work of sanctification is God's work, not ours. We are delivered through our troubles, and find life in the hard times as we draw near to God. If we truly believe this, we are better able to accept those things in our life that make us uncomfortable, knowing that abundant life comes from our journey and not our point of departure. As God's ambassadors, we interact with people who are lost, and know that it is in our outpouring of our love for the gospel that we find ourselves.

A Prayer to Remember

God . . .

Grant me the serenity, calmness, and will,
to accept what I can't seem to change
Remove from my heart the lack of acceptance,
and give me your peace in exchange

Remind me that you are the one who's in charge,
when I don't like the things that are odd
Help me, dear God, to give it to you—
the One inimitable God

Grant me the courage to change what I can,
depending on help from your Son
I may have to just walk away from "things" . . .
and sometimes I may have to run

I may need to keep silent, or maybe speak out . . .
and I know I must swallow my pride
Help me, dear Lord, tap into the strength,
Of your Spirit that is living inside

And please, Lord, give me your wisdom . . .
That I'll know what I can or can't do
The wonderful, powerful, copious wisdom . . .
That no one can give me but you

This is a prayer that will guide me . . .
And will help me to make the right choice
So I won't think that I know the answer . . .
But will wait upon hearing your voice

Help me, dear God, to remember this prayer,
and reflect on it throughout the day
Your serenity, courage, and wisdom . . .
Will truly enlighten my way

Be a Good Citizen

So give back to Caesar what is Caesar's, and to
God what is God's.

(Matthew 22:21)

One of the challenges we have in helping men transition out of prison is helping them think differently. Many men have been in prison a long time and are very aware that life is short. They have families to shepherd, careers to establish, and college degrees to finish. It's time for them to tell others that they have changed and have learned from their mistakes. It's time for them to be there for others, and to chart a course without the constraints of prison.

Unfortunately, pursuing these goals isn't easy. A person can't be there for someone else unless that person lets them. They can't establish their careers without someone willing to employ them, and they won't employ them until they come to know that they are reliable and honest. They can't finish their degrees without spending time and money hitting the books. All of these point to the reality that not being in prison does not mean that we are free of constraints. Leading a successful life requires all of us to acknowledge the constraints in our lives and to not think we are above them.

For by the grace given me I say to every one of you:
Do not think of yourself more highly than you ought,
but rather think of yourself with sober judgment, in
accordance with the measure of faith God has distributed to each of you. (Romans 12:3)

The advice given in this Bible passage provides Christian instruction for thinking differently: 1) by not thinking of ourselves too highly; 2) by having sober judgment; and 3) by thinking of ourselves in accord with our faith. Following this advice helps us become good role models.

Almost everyone thinks more highly of themselves than they should. It's easy to slip into thinking that if we had been given a fair chance then life would be different. This perspective is pervasive in America where television shows life that is simple and good, but the reality is that our lives are a mess. We want what they have—a caring family, nice clothes, a house, friends who are loyal and supportive—but often have just the opposite. If men don't have a persecution complex before they go to prison, it is certainly established in prison, as inmates have to answer to the guards.

Feeling persecuted is a form of institutionalism that works against becoming an ambassador. While its roots may lie in the feeling of not being valued, it often expresses itself in an opposite way when a person either doesn't want to, or can't, follow the rules. Responsible citizens obey laws, pay taxes, report crimes, and generally try to live within the constraints of society for the betterment of themselves and others. People who are institutionalized have a me-versus-them mentality where breaking the rules is OK as long as you don't get caught, shading the truth is

OK if the lie is against "them," and not stepping up to do your fair share of the work is OK because someone else will do it.

Getting rid of an institutionalized mindset and not thinking of yourself too highly is difficult, because prison is a traumatic experience. It is easy to relive traumatic experiences and become self-centered. I was recently at the dentist to have some cavities filled, and asked the dentist to make sure to use plenty of novocaine. I absolutely hate having fillings at the dentist because of the chance of experiencing pain in my mouth. When I asked about the novocaine the dentist said that everyone my age says the same thing. It seems that dentists did not use enough novocaine to fill cavities in the 1960s, and a whole generation was traumatized.

I don't think this trauma of mine is anything like the trauma other people experience in life, especially if they have been to prison. The horrible conditions that are present in prison reinforce the idea of failure and institutionalism. The guards don't have degrees in psychology or sociology and can't adequately respond to the needs of inmates. Inmates often don't respect each other and routinely get into fights to exploit one another. They are given horrible food to eat and medical care is minimal. Some of the men who come to us don't even have loved ones who would visit or write them during their entire incarceration. It is easy to see how a person can conclude that no one cares about them. It's easier to think that someone is out to get them, because then at least they have some value and matter to someone in some way.

The only way out of this mindset is to believe that God loves each one of us, and that by identifying with Christ's death on the cross we are able to stand rightly with our Creator. Our rights are given up in this process as we take on the righteousness of

Christ, and we walk with Him in a foreign world as an ambassador. In this process we can accept that people are not out to get us as individuals, but that the social system is flawed and imperfect. In an effort to save money, cheap food is served, and old, less effective medicine is prescribed. Counseling sessions are staffed by people who are often tired and just doing their jobs, and who may be institutionalized themselves. Identifying with Christ gives us the ability to break the mindset of being persecuted for anything other than being a Christian. Allowing grace to come into our lives allows us to admit our sins and not think too highly of ourselves, as we take on the realization that "but for the grace of God go I."

Some of the men coming into our ministry have identified their lives with Christ and are ready to serve. One man almost immediately went back into a juvenile detention center in Columbus to speak to the youth about the choices they were making and the likely result of these choices. The youth accepted his words and the man felt great about having the chance to make a difference in their lives. This man had his sight set on serving God and he prospered after his incarceration. Other men come out with chips on their shoulders and don't do so well.

The second lesson from Romans 12:3 is thinking of ourselves with sober judgment. Christians need to realize that they are made in the image of God and able to respond to God. They are filled with the Holy Spirit who is at work though them. What they do with their lives matters because they know that they are part of God's plan.

Thinking like an ambassador means that we need to stop thinking in small, immediate terms and instead think more broadly, and with a longer perspective. It requires us to develop tools for the kingdom rather than spend our time playing with the toys of this world. We need to reach out to others rather than be comfortable in our own lives. And, we need to start playing seek-and-save rather than hide-and-seek.

Some men coming from prison are materialistic. They want to buy stuff and acquire things. We know this is happening because storage space at our ministry houses is limited and it's easy to notice the accumulation. When these men get jobs and get paid, they deposit money into the house savings program and then spend every remaining cent that they have. They are usually broke around payday, and continue to bump along from paycheck to paycheck although they don't have to; we don't charge rent and there is plenty of food in the house.

Finally, we are called to think of ourselves in accord with the measure of faith God has given. It is best to think of our measure of faith in terms of the spiritual gifts that God has given to us. God blesses each of us differently, and calls us to be members of His church where we are to work together. Part of having genuine maturity involves understanding the spiritual gifts God has given us, taking them seriously, and using them for God. While people of the world compete to surpass each other, mature Christians desire to use whatever grace and work God gives them to bless others.

Send Me, Lord . . . I'll Go!

God has a job for all of us
He gave us special skill
He made us good at *something*
To use it for His will

He doesn't look at circumstance
To Him it matters not
So put your gifts to use for *Him*
And give it all you've got

Turn away from yesterday
Be strengthened by your fall
Be willing to *think* differently
And listen to His call

Stand up against the enemy
Do not invite him in
Exemplify your faith in God
Don't put your faith in men

Ignore those who may tell you,
"For *you* God has no use.
You're a loser. You're a failure.
You no longer can produce!"

The devil is a liar . . .
Not a word he says is true
God can use our troubles
And He's calling out to you

He has a special job for you
That you may not yet know
If only you'll respond by saying,
"Send me, Lord . . . I'll go"

Discussion Questions

1. What are some big constraints in your life? Which are hardest for you to live with?

2. When was the last time you stood up for your rights? Would Christ have done the same thing?

3. What small miracles have you seen lately?

4. Where do you cut corners when it comes to giving to Caesar?

5. Is there anything that offends you? Do you think Christ was offended by this?

6. What is the measure (i.e., nature) of your faith?

7. Who are the "us" and "them" in our society? How can you help people reach out to the "them" of society?

8. How can you help people see the example they are setting?

Chapter 11

BE GOD'S AMBASSADOR

What I (Timothy) have learned in my walk with Christ since I accepted Him in September 1976 is that His desire is to reproduce Himself in us. My experience has taught me that walking with Him needs to be in a triangular form, i.e., to have fellowship with Him (vertical) all the time as well as having fellowship with others (horizontal).

Jesus is a Spirit; He can move the way He wants, and He can reach people the way He wants. But all the time, He wants to involve us in reaching His people. In other words, He wants fellowship with us and then to send us into the world, to have fellowship with those whom we bring to Him.

Fellowship is a godly thing; it proves how we are parts in the body of Christ. All the time when people meet for fellowship, the spirit of joy and oneness comes down and overshadows them. When I think of fellowship, I remember the fellowship with Greg and the ex-prisoners at Fort Jackson; I always feel the presence of the Holy Spirit hovering over us. You can openly see how the faces around the table glimmer, and everyone being so live and active bringing the presence of God down and connecting us together, to a point that we do not feel ready to leave the place. God is the initiator of our fellowships with Him and His people.

Fulfilling the Great Commission is not a denominational or a church thing but a personal commission. It is one of the indications whether Christ lives in you, as a born-again Christian. It should be a passion, an impulse driving a saved Christian from the inside out. I remember one day at about 7:30 p.m. East African Time, Matthew at Singida got saved. In no time, Matthew went out straight from where we were to one of the bishops' houses and knocked on the window, saying, "Bishop, wake up, you need to accept Jesus as your personal savior."

To his surprise, he was apprehended by the bishop's security guard and sent to the police outpost for causing tension in that place without permission. Soon enough, the bishop heard about it and called the police to release him. The following day, the man asked for an appointment to meet with the same bishop and his request was accepted. He met with the bishop and told him about accepting Jesus Christ as his personal Savior. Matthew found himself fulfilling the Great Commission by being driven by the fire of the Holy Spirit that was blustering in him, immediately after he received Jesus Christ.

The Great Commission is what makes the church exist. The purpose for our existence is to reach the world with the Word of God. Our church motto is, "Till the Whole World Comes to Jesus." Our joy and satisfaction are when we do missions work, going to the unreached rural communities, preaching the Word and planting churches. We started this in 2009 and by now we have planted churches in six rural areas. The last one we planted was in Bukoba, around Lake Victoria, in February 2019.

I see my brother Greg and his wife Tricia fulfilling the Great Commission by reaching prisoners with the saving Word of Jesus Christ. They also have two ex-prisoners' outposts where they host those who have come out of jail, some after serving in jail for twenty-five years. They minister to them, bringing them back to Christ and reuniting them with their spouses, families, and relatives at all costs. I have been to both outposts (Fort Jackson and the Covenant House) and it is amazing; one cannot believe how Greg and Tricia minister to those neglected people. However God, who loves those ex-prisoners, looked for people who would be ready to fulfill the Great Commission by reaching them, and he found Greg and his lovely wife Tricia. These are great servants of God.

I always tell my brother Greg, "I am a pastor, I deal with people. But the main difference between my mission and yours is that I deal with people who are sober, people who want to excel from good to better. With you, brother Greg, it is different; you deal with people who have lost hope, people who despair, people who have given up, people who are no longer accepted by the community." However, that is the call Greg and his beautiful wife Tricia received from God to do and they are doing it perfectly! Recently, one of the ex-prisoners was officially ordained as a pastor and he is ministering in a neighboring church (Second Chance Church) just across the road from Fort Jackson. Praise, honor, and glory be to the Most High God, the Almighty.

Ambassadors work in fellowship to fulfill
the Great Commission.

Be in Fellowship

> *[I pray] that all of them may be one, Father, just as you
> are in me and I am in you. May they also be in us so
> that the world may believe that you have sent me.*

(John 17:21)

Being an ambassador means being called into fellowship with
Christ, where we find our identity and purpose. When we are
joined with others who are like-minded the experience is powerful. With Christ, I (Greg) can meet someone for the first time
and know that it will be easy to like them, to work with them, to
learn from them and to teach them, to give to them and receive
from them. Being an ambassador means that we are in the presence of God and that we represent God.

Sunday mornings for men in our ministry involves a trip
downtown to volunteer at the breakfast ministry where it all
began. The men take turns cooking eggs, pouring coffee, and
picking up trash. The best job is sitting at tables talking with the
people who come in for a meal and some clothing. It takes a while
to learn how to ask questions so that people aren't suspicious of
what you want, but a simple question like "How has your week
been?" can open up a conversation where everyone is blessed.

The fellowship of Christians is a wonderful experience where
we focus on others. Our individuality is surrendered when God
touches our heart, and we all want the same thing—to draw
close to God by engaging in ministries of service. The community of believers is uplifting in their kingdom work:

> Finally, brothers and sisters, whatever is true, whatever
> is noble, whatever is right, whatever is pure, what-
> ever is lovely, whatever is admirable—if anything is

excellent or praiseworthy—think about such things. (Philippians 4:8)

I am blessed to be part of a men's ministry where our house managers are aware of the importance of men living in harmony (Psalm 133). The fellowship among the men in the houses is strengthened by nightly devotions and a sincere desire to better oneself.

In fellowship we can be ourselves, supported by our brothers in Christ. We can be sharpened, challenged, gain understanding, edified, instructed, comforted, encouraged, made to feel valuable, appreciated, strengthened, taught, and counseled. At the same time, we support, sharpen, challenge, understand, edify, instruct, comfort, encourage, value, appreciate, strengthen, teach, and counsel others. It is clear when a man's presence at the house is negative, and unfortunately the presence of a negative influence has a bigger impact on group morale than a positive influence of equal magnitude (Haggai 2:12–14). It is important that God's embassies remain consecrated, and we fellowship to strengthen ourselves and edify others.

Why We Fellowship

We come together to fellowship . . .
    to share what God has done
To identify with Jesus Christ,
    His one and only Son

We come together and meet the folks
    that God wants us to know
Folks like us, but different . . .
    we can help each other grow

Folks that we can learn from . . .
    and folks that we can teach
Folks to help us stay within
    the Holy Spirit's reach

We come together to fellowship
    as we praise our God above
We come together and learn
    about His unconditional love

We do not meet to pamper
    those who pat us on the back
We do not meet to judge those
    who have fallen off the track

We do not meet to applaud ourselves
    and brag about our "calling"
We meet to honor the only one
    who *can* keep us from falling

God wants for us to know Him
    and to understand His will
And to keep our pride and selfishness
    from taking us downhill

Fellowshipping plays the role
    of keeping us in tune
Preparing us to meet our Lord,
    who is coming very soon

God wants for us to fellowship
    with each other . . . you and me
We need often come together . . .
    to express why we are free

We need to give our testimonies;
>   we need to tell our story
How God has turned our lives around
>   and how we give Him glory

We come together to honor God
>   and listen as He speaks
Sunday mornings, Wednesday evenings,
>   and often through the weeks

Assembling of the saints is something
>   we all are called to do
Let's honor what God has asked . . .
>   and meet together, me and you

Let us come together more often
>   as this new year takes its course
And let the fellowshipping with *God*
>   be our #1 resource

God is in each one of us . . .
>   we bring Him when we meet
And if we agree together . . .
>   we will never face defeat!

Fulfill the Great Commission

> *Therefore go and make disciples of all nations,*
> *baptizing them in the name of the Father and*
> *of the Son and of the Holy Spirit.*

(Matthew 28:19)

My wife and I were visiting my hometown a few years ago and were having lunch with my brother and sister-in-law. We both had moved away from Cleveland after we got married—my brother moving to New England for schooling and to start a family, and my wife and I moving to Chicago to do the same. It was a little strange being back in town. I grew up in an ethnically diverse part of Cleveland, going to a high school that was about a third Jewish, a third Catholic, and a third Protestant. I like living in Columbus but miss the different cultures.

We were reminiscing about high school days, and the topic eventually came around to what our lives would have been like if we would have stayed in Cleveland. It's hard to imagine something like that because we all get caught up in the lives we live now. Trying to imagine what life might have been if we had done something else usually leads to an unrealistic assessment of our potential. None of us has any idea of what God specifically intends for us, and it is too easy to claim victory for the few things we've done right and that we choose to remember or imagine.

Reaching our potential isn't about us being satisfied with how our lives have turned out. I don't think it is about being rich or poor or a leader or anything like that. I don't think it is about what we've done in the past. Instead, I think it is about a state of being—being where God wants us to be, when He wants us to be there, doing what He wants us to do.

Whether I stayed in Cleveland or not certainly would have affected me in many ways—possibly the job I have today, the wife I have today, the family I have today, the organizations I'm involved in today, and so on. Staying in my hometown would have affected many worldly aspects of my life, but it really doesn't speak to my reaching my potential.

The Westminster Catechism speaks to the issue of our potential. It was written in 1647 by English and Scottish theologians to educate people in matters of doctrine and belief, and is considered to be one of the greatest statements to come out of the English Reformation. The Catechism is organized along simple questions and answers. The first question is "What is the chief end of man?" In other words, "What is the purpose of our lives?" The answer to this question affects our assessment of our potential, particularly whether we are on the right path and moving in the right direction. The answer to the first question is, "Man's chief end is to glorify God (Psalm 86) and to enjoy Him forever (Psalm 16)."

It is useful to think seriously about how we measure up to this answer. If you are like me, I think I'm doing a pretty good job of enjoying God, but I'm not doing so great when it comes to glorifying Him. We enjoy God in many ways—we know that God is our shepherd and cares for us. He is the perfect Father. He is perfect in love and in justice. We don't have to worry about who wins in the end, and we don't have to worry about settling the score against those who sin against us because we have assurance that He has our back. We love it when the Holy Spirit moves within us and among us during worship. Our souls sing for God, and occasionally we are given glimpses of perfection. I marvel at the perfection of the Bible and am in awe of how a document can be so perfectly intertwined and consistent in its message despite being written by forty human authors over a period of 1,500 years on three different continents. I see the Bible as a literal miracle.

I'm much further from my potential when it comes to glorifying God. I don't pray enough, and I don't forgive as readily as I should. I often lack the heart that God wants me to have, and it is painful for me to realize that.

Faith is made complete when our head, heart, and hands come together to honor and glorify God. Some of us are predisposed to use our heads when we worship. For us, our goal is to take what we know about God, through His written Word, into our hearts and express it with our hands. For others who are predisposed to sensing God with their hearts, the goal is to ground our feelings in Scripture and to employ more rational thought in the decisions of our lives. A third group of us are good at doing work, but need help getting our heads and hearts focused on God and not ourselves.

The Westminster Catechism reminds us that we exist to glorify God and to enjoy Him. We accomplish this with the help of the Holy Spirit, knowing that we all fall short of our potential, knowing that our faith is expressed continually and is not something that is ever accomplished. We can be God's ambassadors at work, on the playing field, in church, in prison, in the classroom, and wherever else we may be in pursuit of His perfection. Ambassadors of God exist in all walks of life.

Great Potential

God made us in His image,
    though the world may not agree
We all have great potential,
    and He wants us all to see

That we're able to do many things . . .
    of which you could not know
You can go beyond the limit
    if you go when God says go

See, God has placed in each of us . . .
     magnificent potential
But it's vital that we learn
       to comprehend it . . . it's essential

We have gifts and skills and talents
       that we do not exercise
We have power from on high
       that we have yet to realize (Luke 24:29)

You *do* have the potential
       to do awesome things . . . for sure
Do you recognize God's gifts to you? . . .
       Do you know what they are for?

It doesn't matter where you're at,
       or what your case may be
Healthy or sick, young or old,
       behind the walls or free

You too! have great potential, friend,
       no matter what your story
God gives us gifts . . . each one of us,
       to use to bring Him glory

He'll call you out from building tents,
       He'll call you out from fishing
He has a better job for you . . .
       He'll show you what you're missing

Moses thought that tending flock
       was all he'd ever do
Joseph thought that also . . .
       they both found it not true

Jeremiah, David, Gideon . . .
    and many others we could name
They learned of their potential . . .
    and could never be the same

So let's not put a limit
    on the things we can achieve
Because "all things are possible,
    if only we believe."

Do you know that you're amazing
    in the things that you can do?
You're a fascinating character
    when God puts His hands on you

God made us in His image,
    and He has a master plan
He gave us *great potential* . . .
    we just need to understand.

Final Words

We hope you have found the description of our experiences interesting and exciting. Embassy work is an important part of our lives and has taught us a great deal. The meaning of the word "love," for example, is greatly enriched when it is applied to people who are from a different walk of life whom you want to treat as a brother or sister in Christ. As their families become your families and their hardships become your hardships, you realize that advice isn't always the greatest thing we can give each other, and that sacrifice truly means putting yourself aside for the sake of someone else's development. As usually happens in any ministry, the servant becomes the receiver and is blessed even more.

We encourage you to give some thought to what heaven might look like—who will be present and what we will be doing there. We will have the chance to meet God, Jesus, and the Saints that we have all read about. Imagine what it will be like to hear first-hand accounts of the Old Testament battles, the Exodus, and early missionary journeys. As these stories are exchanged it will eventually become our turn to share about our experiences and battles for Christ. Take time today to think about what you will say. It might be time for you to more fully engage in Kingdom work if you feel that you aren't currently doing enough.

Discussion Questions

1. Where do you experience Christian fellowship?

2. What do you get out of fellowship?

3. Do you wish you lived somewhere else? Why?

4. How do you glorify and enjoy God?

5. What stories do you plan to tell about your life on Earth once you reach heaven?

6. What are you doing to encourage fellowship with others at your church or in your community?

7. What is the hardest part of taking criticism? How can you best give criticism?

8. How can we, as a community of faith, more intentionally fulfill the Great Commission?